SpringerBriefs in Economics

More information about this series at http://www.springer.com/series/8876

Andrzej Piotr Wierzbicki

The Future of Work
in Information Society

Political-Economic Arguments

 Springer

Andrzej Piotr Wierzbicki
National Institute of Telecommunication
Warsaw
Poland

ISSN 2191-5504 ISSN 2191-5512 (electronic)
SpringerBriefs in Economics
ISBN 978-3-319-33908-5 ISBN 978-3-319-33909-2 (eBook)
DOI 10.1007/978-3-319-33909-2

Library of Congress Control Number: 2016939055

Printed on acid-free paper

This Springer imprint is published by Springer Nature
The registered company is Springer International Publishing AG Switzerland

Acknowledgments

The author would like to express his deep gratitude to the reviewers, Profs. Bogdan Galwas and Elżbieta Kryńska, as well as to the internal reviewer, Dr. Maria Wierzbicka, for their very incisive and useful reviews. Comments of an anonymous reviewer in Springer Verlag also contributed significantly to the final version of this book.

Contents

About the Author

Andrzej Piotr Wierzbicki was born on June 29, 1937 in Warsaw. He graduated with a Master degree in Engineering in the field of Automatic Control in 1960 from the Warsaw University of Technology, the Faculty of Telecommunications. During 1958–1961, he worked at the National Electrotechnology Institute. Between 1961 and 2004, he worked at the Warsaw University of Technology, first in the Chair for Automatic Control (later renamed as an institute, and operating today as the Institute of Automatic Control and Applied Computer Science) of the Faculty of Telecommunications, later renamed as Faculty of Electronics, and since 1995 known as the Faculty of Electronics and Information Technology. He obtained a doctoral degree at the Faculty of Electronics in 1964, a Doctor of Science (habilitation) in 1968, the title of Professor in 1976, the position of tenured professor in 1992. During 1976–1978, he was the Dean of the Faculty of Electronics of the Warsaw University of Technology. In the period 1979–1984, he held the position of the Chairman of the Systems and Decision Sciences Program of the International Institute for Applied Systems Analysis in Laxenburg near Vienna, Austria. During 1991–1994, he was elected as the Chairman of the Commission of Applied Research of the State Committee for Scientific Research of Poland. He worked at different universities in different parts of the world, e.g., in Japan (in 1989–1990 at the Kyoto University, and in 2004–2007 in the Japan Advanced Institute of Science and Technology in Nomi near Kanazawa). From 1996 until now, he has been working at the National Institute of Telecommunications in Warsaw, and during 1996–2004 he served as the Director General of this Institute.

He has published dozens of scientific books, over 150 papers in scientific journals or chapters in books, over 120 papers at scientific conferences, and is an author of several patents, including three implemented and broadly utilized. He was a scientific supervisor of over 20 doctoral theses, several of his former doctoral students (A. Dontchev, I. Lasiecka, A. Lewandowski) are professors in different universities in different parts of the world, and many others—professors at Polish universities.

He has contributed to the theory of control and optimization—he is, *inter alia*, the author of the maximum principle for processes with delays, optimization algorithms used for shifted penalty functions and augmented Lagrange functions with generalizations for dynamic optimization and constraints in a Hilbert space. He also authored a generalized approach to the theory of sensitivity of dynamic systems and optimal control, based on the distinction between a basic model and a perturbation model as well as on a structural version of the implicit function theorem (a monograph, in Polish and also in English).

His main contribution is the authorship of an original approach to the theory and methodology of vector optimization, multiple criteria decision support and design. This approach, called *reference point method*, in the theoretical layer is based on new characterizations of vector optimal solutions using conical separations of sets and a specific class of achievement (scalarizing) functions, parametrically dependent on a reference point. In the methodological layer, the approach stresses *the sovereignty of a user of decision support system* or a design support system (who should be supported and not replaced by an automatic choice of a decision or a design variant). This approach achieved an international recognition and became a basis of further research of many authors (in the USA, Europe, and Japan).

Andrzej P. Wierzbicki worked also on the game theory and negotiation techniques. More recently (1997), he proposed a *rational evolutionary theory of intuition*, based on information theory and the distinction between the difficulty of processing of verbal information and immanent information (full information reaching a human by all senses, but mostly visual) and the recognition of the simplifying and accelerating role of the evolutionary invention of speech as opposed to intuition. This theory suggests that at most 0.01 % of human neurons are involved in rational, verbal, and logical thinking. During 2004–2007, he also worked in Japan on micromodels of knowledge creation and co-edited two monographs on this theme.

Since 1985, he has cooperated closely with the Future Studies Committee "Poland 2000 Plus" of the Polish Academy of Sciences, serving, *inter alia*, as the scientific secretary and later, as an editor of the journal *Przyszłość: Świat, Europa, Polska (Future: World, Europe, Poland)* issued by this committee. He has also authored many publications concerning the development of *information society* and *informational* or *knowledge civilization*. His recent book (2015), *Techne$_n$: Elements of Recent History of Information Technologies with Epistemological Conclusions* is also related to this theme.

He was granted many international and Polish awards and distinctions, among them are:

- 1991: *Georg Cantor Award* of the International Society on Multiple Criteria Decision Making, Taipei, Taiwan;
- 2000–2002: Selected by the European Commission as a member of ISTAG (Information Society Technology Advisory Group), Brussels, Belgium;
- 2003: Belgian distinction for inventiveness, Le Merite De L'invention, Croix d'Officier, No. 1819, Brussels, Belgium;
- 2005: *Best Paper Award* of the 38th Hawaii International Conference on System Science, Kulualoa, Hawaii;
- 2006: Distinguished with *T. Hofmokl Award* for the popularization of the ideas related to the information society and the promotion of computer network development in Poland, Warsaw.

Chapter 1
Introduction

Abstract This chapter indicates main themes of the book: the causes of and the responsibility for growing unemployment and social inequality. The author, a technologist, admits that a part of the causes belongs to technology, but most causes result from the capitalist system. This system includes a mechanism of capital replacing labour (actually, investments in technology replacing labour), and this mechanism contains a positive feedback, accelerating such replacement (the more a capitalist earns by such replacement, the more similar investments follow). Such investments occur today at unprecedented scope and speed and this is the main cause of resulting social troubles. The chapter includes also a short review of related literature.

Keywords Escalating automation · Capital replacing labour · Acceleration by a positive feedback · Growing unemployment · Growing inequalities · Endangered capitalism

I was motivated to write this book by the feeling of co-responsibility for disturbing socio-economic phenomena related to the utilization of high technology by the contemporary capitalistic system. By profession, I am a specialist in automatic control and informatics, and have been working in this field for over 50 years. Over 40 years ago I took part in automation of Polish steelworks and sugar plants in the hope that this would help people in their hard work. Today, however, I observe how the escalating automation and robotization of all work, including intellectual work, results in growing unemployment and increasing social inequality. Thus, I ask myself: are we, automatic control specialists, responsible for these phenomena?

I answer myself: indeed, to some extent, since we did not forecast with sufficient precision the social effects of universal automation and robotization. It was predicted by Lem, e.g. in his novel of science fiction, *Return from the Stars* (Lem 1961)—even if his book did not analyze seriously enough the social consequences of automation.[1] I know that among Polish politicians there was one, Adam Rapacki, who anticipated the same at that time and offered me then a private opinion that automation will lead to a destruction and loss of importance of proletariat—and he was right (see Chap. 4). Later, such situation was also envisaged by Toffler in the book *The Third Wave* (Toffler 1980), who precisely predicted the nature of informational revolution even if his interpretation of the history of civilizations was imprecise (the number of waves was much higher than three, e.g., the civilization before Gutenberg was quite different than after Gutenberg, see e.g. Braudel 1979). However, all these generally correct predictions were not precise enough and we, control, robotic and computer engineers, were still designing new tools and technologies enabling automation, in the hope that this would make the life of people easier.

On the other hand, new tools and technologies can be diversely utilized and it is precisely the way of their utilization that defines the responsibility for the consequences. If a driver uses a car to kill people, who is responsible: the designer of the car or the driver? This does not mean that tools are neutral by nature; they can exert individual or social fascination with sometimes catastrophic results, see (Heidegger 1954). Nevertheless, it is the social system of their utilization that responsible for this, see (Wierzbicki 2011). The economic mechanism of growth of unemployment and social inequality is simple: *since capitalists are motivated by profit, when technology gives them the tools reducing the cost of work, they will eagerly use them, increase their yields, decrease costs of work, and thus—also increase inequality.* The problems of *the end of work* and *the increase of inequality* must be, therefore, examined jointly. Moreover, we are all responsible: if we recognize flaws in the socio-economic system of utilization of technology, we should think how to counteract them. Socio-economic systems are also subject to evolution, sometimes slow, sometimes revolutionary, and we should all influence the directions of this evolution by exercising our democratic freedoms. This is obviously a political problem, but also an ethical one that will be discussed in more detail in the next chapter.

Nevertheless we, the creators of information technologies, should feel especially responsible—for two main reasons. Firstly, our further work on the development of technologies might be used for advanced automation, in particular of intellectual work, e.g., we work on the problems of *knowledge engineering*, (see e.g. Granat and Wierzbicki 2009). With our experience in research on automation and robotization (in my own case, as already mentioned, over 50 years of such experience), we can clearly imagine what will be achieved in this field within the next 50 or even 150 years.

---

[1]Lem envisaged a society without work, but did not specify precisely how the problems of distribution and redistribution will be solved in this society. Before Lem, two writers addressed seriously the social consequences of automation: Wiener (1948) and Pollock (1957). Both of them, however, hoped that future society will find new employment ways. The same I hoped even in 2000, when I wrote on the megatrends of information society (Wierzbicki 2000), with one megatrend motivating the change of professions. However, I observe today that automation occurs simply too fast and people would have to change professions too many times during lifetime.

Secondly, several of us intensively collaborate with the Committee of Future Studies to the Presidium of the Polish Academy of Sciences "Poland 2000 Plus" (in my own case, for over 30 years). Our own papers on the informational revolution (e.g. Wierzbicki 2000)—turned out to be accurate and precise, although we encountered initially the so-called *Cassandra effect* (the more precisely somebody forecasts future events, the less credibility is given to such forecast) and this book will probably also encounter this effect. However, we predicted correctly three megatrends of informational revolution: the technical megatrend of *digital integration* (so-called convergence, digitalization of information technologies, integration of media etc.), the social megatrend of *dematerialization of work* (precisely as a consequence of automation and robotization), and the intellectual megatrend of *changing the way the world is perceived* (resulting from the change of basic concepts introduced by information technologies, see also Wierzbicki 2011). Thus, I hope that we can forecast also more far-reaching consequences of the informational revolution.

I believe that—for these two reasons—it is our ethical duty to analyze the future of work in the perspective of the next 50 or even 150 years, and analyze necessary or anticipated modifications of the socio-economic system of utilization of advanced technology.

Firstly, however, I should explain some concepts used in such analysis. The first of them is the already mentioned concept of a *megatrend*. It was introduced by Naisbitt (1982) to denote new great directions of changes influencing our lives. Personally, I stress in this concept that megatrends are *long-lasting* and *interdisciplinary*. We could include to megatrends also the *long-duration waves of social diffusion of new types of technology products*, e.g., electrification, telephony, television—namely the three first waves of informational revolution: personal computers, mobile telephony, Internet, and then the next three waves, already initiated but not yet prevalent, of robotics, knowledge engineering (called popularly artificial intelligence or the Internet of things), and biomedical engineering. Such waves are long-lasting (see Wierzbicki 2011): from an invention to the beginning of actual social diffusion we need usually 40–50 years, while the process of social diffusion is in a sense inevitable, but lasts another 40–50 years. However, in order to distinguish these waves from other megatrends, we shall speak about *subsequent long-duration waves of informational revolution*.

Precisely because of this long-term character, forecasting in the perspective of 50 years can be rather precise, since the dynamics of social diffusion, once it is started, is slow but in a sense inevitable. The mobile cellular telephony was invented in 1943, and even in 1970 people did not have radio-telephones commonly, because they were too heavy (the popularly called 'telephone bricks') and expensive. A wide-spread social diffusion of cellular telephony started after 1990, and still today it does not encompass all of the Polish or global society, but we cannot stop this process of social diffusion. In relation to an earlier wave of television (TV was invented around 1925 but its social diffusion started around 1960), in the year 1967 Guy Debord introduced the concept of *society of the spectacle* (Debord 1967) and gave a critique of its negative aspects, but it did not influence in any way the social spread of television. Such processes of social diffusion are relatively fast, with the maximal speed of increase of circa 8 % of population per year (in one country; the process is obviously slower on a global scale and close to saturation, e.g. it is estimated that in 2013, already 80 % of world population had access to television and there are predictions that the figure will increase to 90 % in 2016, which means an increase of only ca. 3 % per year). Other social diffusion processes, e.g. the process of increase of participation of young people in tertiary education, are slower, and due to demographic reasons the growth processes related to participation of people with tertiary education in a society are even slower—also circa 8 %, but for a decade.

For these reasons, such processes can be rather precisely forecasted. Moreover, many automatic control engineers specialized in the control of processes with delays and understand their dynamics well. Therefore, if *robots* do not walk with us on the streets, and do not serve us in supermarkets, this might be so during next 50 years. If new achievements in knowledge engineering (called imprecisely artificial intelligence or the Internet of things) make it possible to almost fully automate intellectual work, then—depending on the socio-economic system of utilization of such possibilities—after 50 years we should expect either a general unemployment and social exclusion causing serious social tensions, or a radical change of the contemporary capitalist system. Since such changes do not occur fast, we need a perspective of 50 or even 150 years, the latter obviously with less precise forecasts.

Another important concept that we shall use is *feedback*, which denotes a reflexive impact of a time stream of effects on a time stream of causes, usually with a certain delay. If the effects support the causes, we call it a *positive feedback* that usually results in an avalanche-like development to a violent end. Hence, it cannot be considered a positive phenomenon. On the other hand, a positive stabilizing impact is exercised by a *negative feedback* when the effects counteract the causes. The most suitable illustration of this distinction is a group of people around a campfire in winter; those that use negative feedback come closer to the fire if they are cold, but away from the fire if they are too hot; those that would use positive feedback would either come closer and closer to the fire and end burned, or come further and further away from the fire and end frozen. Both types of feedback are broadly used in technology: positive feedback in computer memories, negative feedback in automatic control and robotics. In technical sciences, there exists a thorough and well developed theory of feedback systems, a fact often not noticed by social sciences. E.g., Soros (2006), following Karl Popper, correctly stresses the fallibility of all theories and the belief in advantages of open society, but he justifies this also by the universality of *reflexivity relation*—mutual interaction of causes and effects—without noting that he speaks actually about *feedback relation*, a phenomenon well and deeper studied earlier in technology.

A danger to human civilization is related to the fact that, as it was shown in (Wierzbicki 2011), there are two loops of positive feedback between science and technology and between technology and market that are the actual reason of the avalanche-like development of human civilization during last 200 years—and such avalanche-like development almost always ends in a violent or sudden impact, hitting some constraint. Such constraint, analyzed in this book, might be the end of work and an excessive increase of social inequalities. The problems analyzed in this book are bothering sociologists and economists and much discussion and publications were devoted to them. Therefore, we shall relate here shortly the recent results of such discussions, as a basis for further analyses.

We shall start with the issue of socio-economic inequalities. Perhaps most incisive in this subject is the recent book of the Noble prize laureate Stiglitz (2012): *The Price of Inequality: How Today's Divided Society Endangers Our Future.* In his book, Stiglitz shows in detail how social inequalities result in distortions, and in a sense corruption of market mechanisms—and how neoliberal economics creates myths that attempt to hide this corruption. For example, such a myth is the assertion that the so-called *elastic labour market* (that is such that capitalists may employ workers on arbitrary conditions) accelerates economic growth, since it actually results in worsened productivity and work quality: people employed for longer periods are more loyal to their employers and work better. Stiglitz presents also a list of reforms indispensable to restore health of capitalism. From my perspective, however, he does not fully acknowledge the corrupting impact of high technology on market mechanisms, and especially the newly intensified *megatrend of minimization of costs of work*, resulting jointly from profit maximization and the *megatrend of dematerialization of work*. I shall further comment on the opinions of Stiglitz further on in this book.

Piketty (2014), in his huge book *Capital in the Twenty-First Century* stresses that financial inequalities started to grow around 1810 (after the beginning of *industrial revolution*), achieved a maximum at the turn of centuries, decreased in the 20th century, but started to grow again around 1980 (together with *informational revolution*, see Wierzbicki 2011); today, the income of the richest class of society grows three times faster than the global GDP. However, Piketty looks for the cause of such phenomena in synthetic economic categories, while an American economic politician, Summers (2014), maintains that the growth of inequalities results from two specific causes: technology development and globalisation. In this respect, I agree with Summers, but I have to say that his analysis is also not sufficiently deep: in order to propose ways of counteracting the mechanisms of inequality growth, we must understand them well. I believe that *the main reason of the growth of inequalities today the megatrend of dematerialization of work used by capitalists to decrease the costs of work*—either through globalization, meaning export of work to less developed countries, or through automation.

Piketty proposes counteracting the growth of inequalities through strongly progressive taxes—and most probably this very suggestion evokes a strong criticism of his book by rightist economists that defend the traditional or neoliberal paradigm of economics (e.g., by using epithets like "Capital in the Twenty-First Century, or mythology for ignorant people"). I agree with Piketty as regards the main direction of action, but disagree as to the details. He does not show how progressive taxation would limit the megatrend of minimization of the work costs, while one specific method, a *degressive taxation depending on an employment index*, is proposed in further chapters of this book.

In the discussions on the book *Capital in Twenty-First Century* a question was raised: *why the increase of inequalities is bad?* This is an ethical question that will be analyzed in the next chapter. On the other hand, from a pragmatic point of view of even the richest classes of society we could answer with a question: *would you want your children or grandchildren to become a target of a global revolution similar to that of 1917, but exploiting the new possibilities of Internet and new weapons, including nuclear ones?* After all, the revolution of 1917 in Russia occurred due to the tremendous increase of socio-economic inequalities during entire 19th century and contributed to their decrease started in the middle of the 20th century. Some capitalists and plutocrats note this danger today: e.g., Hanauer (2014) writes *The Pitchforks Are Coming for Us, Plutocrats*, even if he does not fully understand the mechanism of the growth of inequalities and believes that it is sufficient to increase the minimal wages in order to limit inequalities.

The literature on the problem of the future of work is also enormous. Among current world-wide publications I should mention the new book of Rifkin (2014), *The Zero Marginal Cost Society*, an author of the earlier *The End of Work* (1995). He presents a vision of the future of work related to the end of capitalism that he predicts as an outcome of the development of the *Internet of Things* (one of the denotations describing future artificial intelligence or knowledge engineering dispersed in the human living environment) and of the collaboration as part of *Collaborative Commons*—but he not fully understands the limitations of these ideas and the power of automation of intellectual work, clearly visible today also in the way the Internet develops. Rifkin provides a correct diagnosis that information technologies result in diminishing marginal production costs,[2] but he discusses only how to counteract monopolistic practices and does not take account of the issue how contemporary capitalism defends itself against diminishing marginal costs by oligopolistic practices consisting in tacit price fixing. I also agree with Rifkin that the development of informational society will result in a further perspective (I believe, during the next 50 or 150 years) in the end of capitalism such as we know it today. However, Rifkin sees such end in a spontaneous social process and does not perceive the dangers of a global revolution. I would like to avoid the revolutionary way; therefore in this book I analyze a possibility of an evolutionary way through democratic reforms.

The analysis by Brynjolfsson and McAffee (2014) in *The Second Machine Age*, written from the perspective of the creators of new information technologies, is more realistic than Rifkin's. They notice correctly that it was the development of technology that resulted in such a spectacular growth of both the population of the world and diverse indicators of social development (a slow slither through thousands of years until around 1800, and today almost vertical incline on such

---

[2]The cost of producing the last additional specimen of a product that, according to the classical economic theory, should define the price on a free market. However, in knowledge-based economy these costs strongly decrease, and prices on high technology markets have lost any dependence on marginal production costs (see Chap. 3). This was noted already by Labini (1962) who has shown that prices on oligopoly markets do not depend on marginal production costs.

historical scale)—but do not see that such processes are a result of positive feed-backs and end inevitably in "hitting the ceiling" which might mean a global catastrophe[3] (see Wierzbicki 2011). Firstly, in their essential conclusions, Brynjolfsson and McAffee correctly emphasize that we live in times of a rapid advancement of information technologies which changes all our ways of life and work (therefore, we use here the concept of *informational revolution*). But further on, they display a hope typical for creators of information technology and maintain that the outcomes of such development will be "profoundly beneficial". They notice, admittedly, that "technological progress is going to leave behind some people, perhaps even a lot of people, as it races ahead", but they do not appreciate the scale of this phenomenon. Nevertheless, they notice that this progress "is going to bring some stormy challenges with it", and even discuss how to meet these challenges, but in their optimism they avoid more radical ones.

A study directly devoted to the future of work is the expertise of Watson and Crosthwaite (2013) *The Future of Work*. The expertise correctly stresses that the nature of work is changing very fast today, "even faster than we think". The authors draw attention to the demographic factors—increasing participation of older people, increasing participation of women in labour force, and they evaluate these trends in the quality of work positively. They point out to the change (increase) of the social significance of work, to the new generation of workers accustomed to the Internet, to the future importance of talent and creativity in work, to the upward trend in the number of part-time workers. They stress also the importance of automation of work, including intellectual work, but the aspects of automation they recognise are mostly positive—such as the possibility of shortening the time of work and lengthening the time of leisure—without addressing the question *how the society will be organized if most of today's work is automated?* Further on, the authors stress the increasing trend in mobile work share, consider how a future place of work should look, point out to network-like changes of the structure of future organizations, the importance of information security, a gradual change from paper to electronic information media. All in all, the expertise they provide is important and acceptable, even if slightly chaotic; nevertheless, it concerns only a few next decades and does not look far enough into the future—where "hitting the ceiling" mentioned earlier lurks.

This problematics is also noted by an influential economic journal, *The Economist*. Over a year ago (April 27 2013) it published an incisive paper on the unemployment of young people, *Generation jobless*, and recently (October 4 2014), a comprehensive special report *The third great wave* on the socio-economic

---

[3]The most simple example of a process with positive feedback is snow avalanche: the more snow it gathers in the beginning, the more it can gather later—until it hits the opposite hillside, which I call here "hitting the ceiling". Another example is a nuclear bomb: the more particles (e.g., of uranium) are destroyed, the more other particles can be destroyed next, until the bomb runs short of particles. In a nuclear power plant the same process occurs, but it is limited by a restrictive negative feedback: if the intensity of nuclear reaction grows too much, the rods controlling this intensity should be inserted deeper; however, if such automatic control system is switched off (e.g. for experimental reasons, as it happened in Chernobyl), a catastrophe will follow.

consequences of the universal use of information technology. However, this has a similar optimistic air to it as the analyses of Brynjolfsson and McAffee (2014); moreover, it is tinged with a neoliberal paradigm typical of this journal.[4]

It is worthwhile to mention the perception of the future of work from the perspective of the socialist movement. Phillips (2014) correctly poses the question "*Are Youth Facing a Future Without Work*", but responds only in an utopist way that it is sufficient to destroy capitalism, and in a socialist society everybody will have work. Since she lacks experience of the so-called real socialism, she does not know that a simplistic organization of socialist society with universal right to work leads usually to market disequilibria, to supply shortages. If the unemployment of young people increases further, then revolutionary ideas will clearly be spreading and can lead even to a *scenario of doom* (see Chap. 6 of this book). However, personally I am more interested in another question: *how to reform and modify capitalism to limit the unemployment of young people?*

There are also several positions concerning the future of work in Polish literature. Most important of them is a collective work, *The Future of Work in the 21st Century* (Borkowska 2004). The book addresses diverse aspects of the future of work in a broader and deeper manner than even the later expertise of Watson and Crosthwaite (2013), *The Future of Work.* For example, in his paper "Globalization and work" Witold Morawski gives an excellent analysis of diverse aspects of globalization and their impact on the future of work. Several papers collected in this book emphasizes also the cultural, social and psychological value of work that supports human dignity. This is a fundamental problem; I believe that people without work not only are socially marginalized, but also internally alienated, and their self-esteem is shattered.

However, similarly as the expertise of Watson and Crosthwaite, *The Future of Work in the 21st Century* approaches the future in the perspective of a few next decades at most. This is understandable—it is a scientific study and science, in its pursuit of objectivity, is afraid of more distant forecasts: see the discussion on the impossibility of precise forecasting (and the necessity of approximate forecasting in civilisation development) in my book (Wierzbicki 2011). Personally, I do not have such inhibitions, since I not only believe that all development of human civilisation is based on approximate forecasts (for example, without such forecasts we could not organize railroad, marine and airplane transport), but also hope that our knowledge of process dynamics lets us forecast correctly. For these reasons, the present book was written—even if it will be not precisely scientific, and rather futurologist, but nevertheless reaching further in the future.

---

[4]By *neoliberalism* we understand here not a variant of *liberalism* (a noble belief that the modern society is founded on respect for individual freedom), but its extreme economic interpretation, a belief that it is sufficient to provide market freedom, and free market will solve every problem. Such belief is evidently propaganda in favour of main market players, since market efficiently solves only the problems that can be easily translated into money, but not those related to higher values: healthy natural environment, justice, objectivity.

Also the futurologist work *Report Poland 2050* (Kleiber et al. 2011) reaches further in the future, as clearly predicts the growth of *precariat*—a new class or part of proletariat including young people: usually well-educated but without job or employed temporarily, on tenuous work contracts. The report forecasts a growing conflict of precariat with the traditional society and economy by posing the question what will be the source of income for precariat if we automate and robotize all production and the profits from this process will be reserved to a narrow class of people. This book in a sense continues the analysis started in the *Report Poland 2050.*

I should also warn the readers that the literature related to the problems discussed in this book is truly enormous and deserves a much deeper scientific treatise. However, the futurology aspects of my book would be lost in such treatise; thus I present instead in this book political-economic essays concerning future, even if scientifically based.

References

Borkowska, S. (Ed.). (2004). Przyszłość Pracy w XXI Wieku. IPiSS, Warszawa 2004. (in Polish: The Future of Work in the 21st Century).

Braudel, F. (1979). *Civilisation matérielle, économie et capitalisme, XV-XVIII siècle.* Paris: Armand Colin.

Brynjolfsson, E., & McAffee, A. (2014). *The second machine age: Work, progress and prosperity in a time of brilliant technologies.* New York: W.W. Norton & Co.

Debord, G. (1967). *The society of the spectacle.* London: Black & Red. (English translation in 1970; rev. ed. 1977).

Granat, J., Wierzbicki, A. P. (2009). Inżynieria wiedzy—nowy obszar badawczy Instytutu Łączności. *Telekomunikacja i Techniki Informacyjne,* 3–4: 108-116. (*Knowledge Engineering—a New Research Area of the National Institute of Telecommunication*).

Hanauer, N. (2014) The Pitchforks are coming … for us Plutocrats. *POLITICOMAGAZINE.* (July/August 2014).

Heidegger, M. (1954). *Die Technik und die Kehre.* In M. Heidegger (Ed.), *Vorträge und Aufsätze,* Günther Neske Verlag, Pfullingen.

Kleiber, M., Kleer, J., Wierzbicki, A. P., Galwas, B., Kuźnicki, L., & Sadowski, Z., et al. (2011). *Raport Polska 2050.* Komitet Prognoz "Polska 2000 Plus" przy Prezydium PAN, Warszawa. (English version *Report Poland 2050* available).

Labini, P. S. (1962). *Oligopoly and technical progress.* Cambridge: Harvard University Press.

Lem, S. (1961). *Powrót z Gwiazd.* Warszawa: Czytelnik. (English translation *Return from the Stars,* Secker & Warburg, London, 1980).

Naisbitt, J. (1982). *Megatrends: Ten new directions transforming our lives.* New York: Warner Books.

Piketty, Th. (2014). *Capital in the twenty-first century.* Cambridge: Harvard University Press.

Phillips, T. (2014). Are youth facing a future without work? *The Socialist Magazine.* (May 24, 2014).

Pollock, F. (1957). *Automation: A study of economic and social consequences.* New York: Fredericks & Praeger, Publishers.

Rifkin, J. (1995). *The end of work: The decline of the global labor force and the dawn of the post-market Era.* Putnam Publishing Group.

Rifkin, J. (2014). *The zero marginal cost society: The internet of things, the collaborative commons and the eclipse of capitalism.* New York: Palgrave Macmillan Trade.

Soros, G. (2006). *The age of fallibility: Consequences of the war on terror.* New York: Public Affairs. (tlum. polskie 2006, *Nowy, okropny świat: era omylności,* Świat Książki, Warsaw).

Stiglitz, J. (2012). *The price of inequality: How today's divided society endangers our future.* New York: Norton & Co.

Summers, L.H. (2014). The inequality puzzle. *Democracy,* (33). (Summer 2014).

Toffler, A. (1980). *The third wave.* New York: William Morrow.

The Economist. (2013). Generation jobless: The global rise of youth unemployment. (April 27th, 2013).

The Economist. (2014). The third great wave. Special report. (October 4th, 2014).

Wiener, N. (1948). *Cybernetics or control and communication in the animal and the machine.* Cambridge: MIT Press.

Wierzbicki, A. P. (2000). Megatrends of information society and the emergence of knowledge science. In *Proceedings of the international conference on virtual environments for advanced modeling.* Tatsunokuchi: JAIST.

Wierzbicki, A. P. (2011). *Techne$_n$: Elementy Niedawnej Historii Technik Informacyjnych i Wnioski Naukoznawcze.* Komitet Prognoz "Polska 2000 Plus" oraz Instytut Łączności (PIB), Warsaw. (English enlarged translation *Techne$_n$: Elements of Recent History of Information Technologies with Epistemological Conclusions,* Springer 2015, Heidelberg).

Chapter 2
Ethical Premises and Values

Abstract This chapter discusses ethical issues related to the main theme of the book: the consequences of a meta-ethical presupposition expressing the concern about future generations. These consequences include justice, sustainable development, but also objectivity treated as fundamental values—perhaps not fully attainable, but motivating our endeavours. Such a perspective resulted in taking up the problems of the future of work and a just social system in an advanced information society in this book. The chapter discusses related ethical problems in detail, ending with a discussion of examples of ethical corruption of markets resulting from possibilities offered by high technology.

Keywords Justice · Sustainable development · Objectivity · Ethics of future of work · Ethics of marketing · Technological possibilities of market corruption

I was motivated to write this book by a meta-ethical presupposition, a supposition of a deeper or rather higher level, from which diverse ethical commandments might result. In this, we should not be afraid of an infinite depth of meta-justifications.[1] There is no sense in looking for even deeper (meta-meta) justifications, if a given meta-ethical presupposition appears sufficiently general and intuitively telling.

Such presupposition expresses my own conviction that *after us, new generations of people will come that will further develop knowledge and civilization, but in conditions of (perhaps even growing) uncertainty concerning future crises and catastrophes, and our ethical beliefs should result from a concern about these future generations.* Many ethical conclusions follow from such presupposition.

---

[1]This infinite depth is called by philosophers *the hydra of infinite regress* and treated as a paradox (since we must use a metalanguage to speak about truth, hence to analyse the truth of the metalanguage we would need a meta-metalanguage, etc.). We should not be afraid of such hydra, since—as it was shown in the book *Techne$_n$* (2011)—robots operate based on an infinite regress in negative feedback loops, and since they actually operate, an infinite regress can be treated as a paradox only in the same sense as the ancient paradox that Achilles will never overtake a turtle.

© The Author(s) 2016
A.P. Wierzbicki, *The Future of Work in Information Society*,
SpringerBriefs in Economics, DOI 10.1007/978-3-319-33909-2_2

The first group of them was noted by Rawls (1971): since we do not have certainty as to the fate of our children and grandchildren, we should leave them possibly most just social relations and ethical precepts, serving them well even in the least favourable conditions; thus, *justice* is a fundamental value. However, this is not the only conclusion; another was noticed by Brundtland (1987) who postulated, in her concept of *sustainable development*, that we should leave to next generations similar conditions and opportunities (mostly concerning natural resources and natural environment) that we had ourselves. The third conclusion was noted in the book Techne$_n$ (2011), supplementing the idea of Rawls: since we do not have certainty about the fate of our children and grandchildren, we should leave them possibly most certain and objective knowledge, helping them to overcome future crises and catastrophes—hence the value of *objectivity*, even if never fully attainable, is nevertheless a fundamental one, similarly as the values of *justice* or *sustainable development*. The fourth conclusion is similar (related to the unattainability of full objectivity), even if further-reaching: since after us next generations will come and further develop knowledge, *it is arrogant and conceited even to maintain that we have reached any absolute truth.* The fifth conclusion is developed in this book: we should utilize and transfer to next generations our knowledge in such a way as to prepare them best for future, predictable crises and challenges. The sixth conclusion—perhaps even a separate, second meta-ethical presupposition—was suggested by Bogdan Galwas: *people have duties not only to next generations; we should care of tolerable life conditions of all other people, perhaps even of all other cohabitants of Earth,*[2] because when we do not care about the present, no care about the future will be effective; moreover, it is unethical to remain indifferent to the extreme stratification and the fate of billions of people in deep poverty.

A reflection on this meta-ethical presupposition resulted from reading an excellent book of Roman Morawski, *Ethical Aspects of Research Activity in Empirical Sciences* (Morawski 2011); I agree with most theses rendered in this book, but the above meta-ethical presupposition results in a subtly different interpretation of ethical questions than presented there.

Roman Morawski has slightly simplified the ideas of John Rawls, without stressing the reference to future generations. And that reference is of fundamental importance, since it allows to interpret ethical problems in terms of evolution of civilizations. Let us consider the following mental experiment: let us ask the question whether old leaders (either individual, or group-wise) of human tribes considered premises similar to John Rawls while giving more or less advanced ethical codes to their tribes? Undoubtedly Moses, when giving the Decalogue to his tribe, was motivated not only by transcendental considerations, but also by pragmatic care about the welfare of this tribe in the future in a similar way as presented in the arguments of Rawls. And the children of this tribe learned ethical precepts from

---

[2] I am aware that this presupposition contradicts e.g. with fighting epidemics caused by viruses (since viruses are also cohabitants of Earth), but it can be also interpreted in the sense of the Buddhist principle *ahimsa.*

parents and teachers who used the Decalogue, forming their ethical personality in that way. This personality was called much later by Kant (1781, 1788) *categorical imperative* or *the moral law within us.*

Thus, ethics is a fundamental element of evolution of civilizations, and hence, it is relative in evolutionary terms: what was ethical behaviour in times of Hammurabi is not necessary ethical behaviour today. On the other hand, ethics is relatively durable in a given historical era, it is a *long-duration phenomenon* as proposed by Braudel (1979, 1995). Moreover, it is not necessarily relative in cultural terms: the ways of development of Christian, Muslim and Buddhist cultures are of course different, but the meta-ethical presupposition presented here is common to all mankind and ethical precepts resulting from it might be similar for all cultures.

It was precisely such a perspective that founded motivation to take up the problem of the future of work in this book, or—more broadly—the problem of a just social system in times after informational revolution, or in an advanced information society. It results from a conviction that an universal application of advanced information technology will change social and economic conditions very profoundly, leading to a new civilization era in which even our views on social justice might change.

From such consideration, many questions of ethical nature emerge.

Firstly, in a 100 or 200 years all production work—either in industry, or in agriculture, but also in mining etc., or even service and administrative work, which is discussed in further chapters of this book—will be automated to such an extent that a small group of specialists will be sufficient for its supervision. If we leave the issues of employment to the free market, then a free market of labour motivated by cost minimization will result in unemployment and social exclusion of the majority of world population. Shall we consider such situation as socially just and acceptable?

Secondly, in all our world we observe slow but inevitable increase of the average duration of human life, which is, of course, a proof of progress (above all in the knowledge and tools used by medicine, but also in the overall level of life and hygiene). The percentage share of people of post-productive age will, therefore, inevitably grow and result in increased costs of retirement systems. Already today, we hear that future retirement benefits should be decreased at least twice. On the other hand, the general increase of prosperity resulted precisely from the work of those elder people, so is it just that they will be discriminated?

Thirdly, contemporary capitalism—more the owners of large corporations than the actual originators of knowledge or art—propagates the concept of *intellectual property rights*: if knowledge and art have become a fundamental productive resource, then allegedly they should be treated as a commodity with a defined property right. The adherents of such a view of knowledge and art do not notice how the concept of intellectual property rights is a double-edged weapon, discrediting the practices of contemporary capitalism if consistently applied. Indeed, we should consider the question: *whose property is the knowledge of methods of automation and robotization of production, services and management?* I have been working to create such knowledge for over 50 years and know well the people who create it; I believe we should be asked to answer this question. My answer is: *this knowledge belongs to all humanity and the profits from the utilization of this knowledge should serve all humanity*—and I know that most of automatic control and robotic specialists will agree with such answer. However, this means that the income (not only profits, rather the total income) from automated production and services should be highly taxed, and this taxation used to provide for a fair life of unemployed and retired people.

Fourthly, another question arises: *is work a fundamental value with an ethical dimension to it?* This is a difficult question since many people avoid work. However, we notice also that work with satisfactory results is an important factor supporting dignity and self-fulfilment of people; people deprived of work feel much inferior. It manifests itself, among other things, in the statistics of suicides in Poland, and their strong correlation with the loss of work. It can be a result of the tradition of industrial society where people loosing work felt socially excluded. However, it is a conviction that has penetrated individual and social subconscious. Therefore, we should admit that work has also an ethical dimension to it, supporting human dignity, self-fulfilment, and might be treated as a fundamental value. But this indicates that among fundamental human rights there is also *the right to work*—even if it should not be treated in absolute, unqualified, as we learned from the lessons of real socialism. Nevertheless, this indicates that *entrepreneurs after informational revolution should be motivated by a new ethical duty: to create new professions and places of work.*

From all such ethical premises, it follows that the contemporary capitalism, if it does not modify essentially its mechanisms, will encounter essential barriers of ethical development as a result of ruthless exploitation of high technology, automation and robotization. These ethical barriers will translate into political problems of deep social unrests and might lead to a global crisis as discussed in one of further chapters here. All this does not mean that I believe obliteration of capitalism is necessary. Capitalism turned out to be a better system than real socialism, even if not ideal, but more resilient to diverse adversities, precisely because it exploits human greed as a fundamental motivation. However, if such is the source of the advantages of capitalism, then—as already noted by Smith (1776)—it is necessary to restrain its mechanisms using ethical premises. And since these are changing—slowly, but inevitably with the development of civilization—we should change also the ways of restricting capitalism.

Many people hold similar opinions to those expressed above. For example, Adam Kalbarczyk, in his interview with *Gazeta Wyborcza* of August 14, 2014, expresses an opinion that "A fundamental difference between the right-wing and the left-wing is the attitude to social change and faith in its sense" and that "One cannot be a leftist conservative nor a rightist supporter of social progress, for such progress means more equality in opportunities and rights for people discriminated until now—for women, minorities and socially excluded—and less religious absolutism in public life." However, I write this book because I have much more experience in automation and robotization, in an assessing their consequences, than most people, as well as in forecasting future—see the quoted books *Techne$_n$* and *Report Poland 2050* (Kleiber et al. 2011)—hence I can more accurately forecast events which are distant in time.

We should also realize that a fundamental assumption not only of right-wing conservatives, but also of centrist neoliberals[3] is the assertion that "everyone is responsible for her/his fate and such people have bigger returns on free market who simply deserve it", but we should not agree with this assertion, since it is unethical (as it follows from the second metaethical presupposition).

A particular consequence of this assertion is *neo-Thatcherism,* an ideology promoting a thesis that each man or woman in future will be a self-employed entrepreneur, thus everybody will have the same chances. This ideology is represented, e.g., by a recent issue of *The Economist* (2015) with editorial papers *Workers on tap* and *There is an app for that,* in which the editors of this neoliberal journal express their delight that digital technology makes it possible for everyone to become an entrepreneur (one of subtitles is *Everyone a corporation*) and that the labour market will be very elastic when larger corporations will simply select workers to specific tasks using short-time outsourcing. This ideology neglects two fundamental aspects. Firstly, the social distribution of talents and entrepreneurship is uneven, hence only a small part of self-employed entrepreneurs will achieve success. Therefore, the economic stratification will further deepen—the more so that high technology requires more knowledge and luck for its successful economic application. Secondly, since there will be less work due to automation and robotization, a majority of those self-employed entrepreneurs will be simply destined to bankruptcy and life in slums.

People that are more capable, talented and entrepreneurial have, in my opinion, also more duties to society—and precisely *the creation of new places of work or even professions becomes such ethical duty of a capitalist in the time after the informational revolution.* The contemporary capitalism should be modified in such a way so that the fulfilment of such duty would be not only an ethical issue—it should also be more profitable (since without such motivation capitalists will not take up that duty).

In the time of informational revolution, there are simply too many possibilities of corruption of the market system, exploiting human greed for unethical profits.

One of the examples of such possibilities is the financial crisis of 2007–2010, which has been, by the way, already called *an ethical crisis of capitalism.* One of the reasons for this crisis was untruthful advertising of the so-called financial derivatives, that is blocks of financial options designed and sold by banks with the assertion of absolute security. Such assertion was based on the utilization of software tools to design them, to compute correlation coefficients of price fluctuations,

---

[3]I value free market as a robust tool of economic equilibration, but I also recognize the fact that slips away in the case of neoliberals. Because of the changes brought by the informational revolution, free market, when left to itself, can be corrupted (because it is based on human greed, and this greed in new conditions can lead to effects not foreseen by the classical market theory, as it happened during the crises 2007–2010, see the example described here and the next chapter).

since according to the classical theory instruments based on uncorrelated options are most secure. Such tools were developed by Lee,[4] an American programmer of Chinese origin, who developed and sold to Wall Street the so-called *copula formula* that enabled fast computation of correlation coefficients. Using this formula, allegedly "absolutely secure" portfolios of financial investments were created— derivatives of derivatives, derivatives of housing markets, etc. The introduction of such "absolutely secure" portfolios inflated the market, and since an average investor could not assess their security himself, he believed in what was advertised. Only a few experts knew that the classical theory assumes the stationarity of the processes of price fluctuations, hence uncorrelated investments are secure only as long as the processes of their fluctuations are stationary—and during a crisis they cease to be.

Thus, we can conclude that the collapse of the financial market was caused by its corruption resulting from greed and from new possibilities offered by informational technology, inaccurately represented in advertisement and thus contributing to the inflation of the investment bubble. Anything could pierce the bubble—and the explanations of neoliberal financial specialists maintaining that the crises resulted from unwise interventions of the USA government are simple excuses, attempts to defend a lost cause. On the other hand, we remember well the division of costs and profits resulting from the crises: costs were borne by small investors, and the entire society in general, and profits went to the owners and managers of the falling banks, in the form of arbitrarily high severances.

This is a clear example of *informational asymmetry* on the market, see also (Stiglitz 2002). Information technologies, on the one hand, simplify general access to information, but on the other hand they can be (and actually often are) utilized to deepen informational asymmetry on the market. It is especially visible in the relation of *the society of spectacle* (Debord 1967) to advertisements. The integration of television with cellular telephony and the Internet strengthens the impact of audio-visual message utilized ruthlessly for advertising—unfortunately untruthful as a rule, transmitting only such information that is favourable for the advertiser, hence increasing informational asymmetry. The receivers of such information are usually aware of this fact, but often do not appreciate the power of its unconscious impact, that Herbert Marshall McLuhan (1964) has very aptly called *the massage of media.*[5]

Other examples and aspects of free market corruption resulting from applications of high technology will be discussed in the next chapter, but one fundamental aspect should be mentioned here: *the oligopolization of high technology markets with tacit price fixing.* The classical market theory assumes that technical progress results in a destruction of all monopolies, but this assumption has become invalid today when knowledge has grown to be a fundamental productive factor. A knowledge-based economy results in a fundamental decrease of marginal production costs: the cost of production of yet another piece of product of the same sort turns

---

[4]See Salmon (2009), under a telling title of *Recipe for Disaster: The Formula That Killed Wall Street.*
[5]McLuhan used a play of words *medium is a massage* instead of *medium is a message.*

out to be minimal in comparison to the costs of preparation of the entire production process, together with the costs of knowledge used for this purpose, see e.g. (Rifkin 2014).

The prices actually observed on high technology markets—either of informational products and services (television, telephone, etc.), or of pharmaceutical products—have lost any relation to the marginal production costs, hence the classical free market theory is not applicable to high-tech markets. This is possible only either in the situation of monopoly—but monopoly is usually restricted by state regulations—or in the situation of oligopoly, where it is much more difficult to uncover tacit price fixing (of a quasi-cartel price fixing, but without open formation of a cartel), see Sylos (1962), Kameoka and Wierzbicki (2005), Wierzbicki (2011). Oligopolies with tacit price fixing became a dominating form of high technology markets.

References

Braudel, F. (1979). *Civilisation matérielle, économie et capitalisme, XV-XVIII siècle*. Paris: Armand Colin.

Braudel, F. (1995). *A history of civilizations*. London, New York: Penguin Books.

Brundtland, G. (Ed.). (1987). *Our common future*. Oxford: The World Commission on Environment and Development, Oxford University Press.

Debord, G. (1967). The society of the spectacle. London: Black & Red. (English translation in 1970; rev. ed. 1977).

Kameoka, A., & Wierzbicki, A. P. (2005). *A vision of new Era of knowledge civilization*. Kobe: Ith World Congress of IFSR.

Kant, I. (1781). *Kritik der reinen Vernunft*. Riga: Johann Friedrich Hartknoch.

Kant, I. (1788). *Kritik der praktischen Vernunft*. Riga: Johann Friedrich Hartknoch.

Kleiber, M., Kleer, J., Wierzbicki, A. P., Galwas, B., Kuźnicki, L., & Sadowski, Z., et al. (2011) *Raport Polska 2050*. Komitet Prognoz "Polska 2000 Plus" przy Prezydium PAN, Warszawa. (English version, *Report Poland 2050* available).

McLuhan, M. (1964). *Understanding media*. London: Ark Paperbacks.

Morawski, R. Z. (2011). *Etyczne Aspekty Działalności Badawczej w Naukach Empirycznych*. Warszawa: Wydawnictwa Uniwersytetu Warszawskiego. (*Ethical Aspects of Research Activity in Empirical Science*).

Rawls, J. (1971). *A theory of justice*. Cambridge: Belknap Press.

Rifkin, J. (2014). *The zero marginal cost society: The internet of things, the collaborative commons and the eclipse of capitalism*. New York: Palgrave Macmillan Trade.

Salmon, F. (2009). Recipe for disaster: The formula that killed wall street. *Wired Magazine* 17.03.2009, Tech Biz: IT.

Smith, A. (1776). An inquiry of the nature and causes of the wealth of nations. London: Strahan and Cadeli.

Stiglitz, J. E. (2002). Information and the change in the paradigm in economics. *The American Economic Review, 92*(3), 460–501.

Sylos, Labini P. (1962). *Oligopoly and technical progress*. Cambridge: Harvard University Press.

The Economist. (2015). *Workers on tap; There is an app for that*.

Wierzbicki, A. P. (2011). *Techne$_n$: Elementy Niedawnej Historii Technik Informacyjnych i Wnioski Naukoznawcze*. Komitet Prognoz "Polska 2000 Plus" oraz Instytut Łączności (PIB), Warsaw. (English enlarged translation *Techne$_n$: Elements of Recemt History of Information Technologies with Epistemological Conclusions*, Springer 2015, Heidelberg).

Chapter 3
Technological Progress in Economics, Market and Democracy Versus Informational Revolution

Abstract This chapter discusses the prevailing opinions in economics concerning the impacts of technological progress on economy and society and shows how the informational revolution and the speed of technological change, caused by positive feedbacks in developmental mechanisms, invalidate today these opinions. After personal computers, mobile telephony and the Internet, quickly integrating together today, next three waves of informational revolution are coming: a social penetration of robots, of knowledge engineering (called imprecisely artificial intelligence) and of biomedical engineering. The coming decades will display changes even more fundamental than the last three decades. The impact of these changes on markets, society, future of work and democracy is discussed in detail.

Keywords Technological progress and unemployment · Dematerialisation of work · Replacement of labour by capital · Coming waves of informational revolution · Tacit price fixing · The value of democracy

The classical economics assumes that technical progress cannot result in a growth of unemployment, because technical progress results in a general increase of welfare, thus also increasing demand, including the demand for labour. The informational revolution, however, together with the mega-trend of *dematerialisation of work* related to it, makes such reasoning invalid. If any work can be automated, then the capitalist system will eagerly exploit this opportunity to reduce production costs by reducing the employment. Historically, this process was more complex and used the opportunities offered by globalisation to transfer harder work to less developed countries, which will be discussed in more detail in the next chapter, but the final result is the global increase of the level of automation of work, and reduction of employment.

And again, the classical economics argues that it is nothing new, that replacing human work by machines has been continuing since the beginning of industrial revolution. True, but this argument is similar to the argument against the concept of knowledge-based economy, saying that production was always based on knowledge. In both cases the scale and speed of events are underrated. Truly, the replacement of labour by capital (or by machines bought by capital) is one of main mechanisms of the development of capitalism since the beginnings of industrial revolution. Luddists protested against it, Babbage, an inventor of mechanical computers, defended (1835) this replacement since it leads to a better division of labour. However, the impact of it on society was slow in these times, in order to adapt it was sufficient to learn and change professions perhaps once in a lifetime. The real problem related to the replacement of labour by capital is that it includes a positive feedback (see Wierzbicki 2015): the more an entrepreneur gains by introducing new machinery, the more (s)he is inclined to invest further in such or similar machinery. However, processes with positive feedback (such as in an avalanche or in a nuclear bomb explosion) always accelerate. Today, the replacement of labour by capital occurs with a speed such that we have to learn continuously and change professions even five times in life. The speed is simply incomparable with the beginnings of industrial revolution.

In the case of knowledge-based economy we note that knowledge becomes today a fundamental, decisive production factor. This leads to a gradual decrease of marginal production costs, as noted e.g. in (Rifkin 2014), and also of actual market prices of products (not necessarily equal to or even determined by these marginal production costs, see the discussion of oligopolization of high technology markets in a further part of this chapter). This results also in a gradual but significant reduction of the costs of work automation and robotisation tools, contributed by the informational revolution.

Let us consider first the example of electronic computers. Invented in 1931 (analog version) and in 1936 (digital version), they turned out to be useful in many different fields, but their broad social penetration started not earlier than in 1977, with Apple 2 introduced by Steven Jobs and Steven Wozniak. Thus, there was a delay of over 40 years from the inventions to the beginning of a broader social penetration. Such a delay was needed to make computers smaller and less expensive (before Apple 2, there were attempts to commercialize computers, but priced at about 50,000 dollars, they were simply too costly; Apple 2 cost was several thousand dollars). Today, after over 40 years as of the beginning of the broad social penetration of personal computers, the process has not yet come to an end in the global scale, but some versions of personal computers—smartphones, tablets, etc.—are that inexpensive that some providers of telecommunication services offer them free while advertising their services.

Other processes of social penetration of the tools of informational revolution are similar. The cellular mobile telephony was invented in 1943, its broad social penetration started around 1990 (attempts to promote mobile telephony date back earlier, between 1970 and 1990 in the USA and Japan, but mobile phones were too expensive then, and too heavy). Today, we witness an integration of mobile telephones and personal computers coupled with a decrease of their prices. We can expect the same with regard to social penetration of robots—they do not walk with us on the streets, nor do they serve us in supermarkets, but they will—or of knowledge engineering software (popularly, but imprecisely called artificial intelligence). Both these inventions are over 50 years old today, but they have not arrived yet at a dawn of a broad social penetration—or rather the beginnings of their social penetration are slow, but soon they will accelerate. As the prices of such tools fall down, we observe an accelerated—much faster than at the beginnings of industrial revolution—substitution of human work by these tools.

Moreover, this process did not result in an equitable growth of welfare, but only in intensified economic stratification. We observe a great increase of incomes of a fraction of percent of the global population, great capitalists whose earnings do not contribute sufficiently to the growth of general demand. This is because at the same time we observe stratification and decrease of income of a large part of the middle class, as well as economic marginalization and social exclusion of a large part of new unemployed or precariously employed young people. And a small increase in general demand does not result in the increase of demand for human labour, since it is cheaper to use automated work. Thus, we can conclude that *the classical capitalist mechanism of profit maximization coupled in a feedback loop with the megatrend of dematerialization of work* (the use of information technology to make the work easier) *transformed into a megatrend of minimization of human labour costs*. In Chaps. 5 and 7, we shall see statistical evidence of this megatrend.

I am not alone in such opinion. The influential economic weekly *The Economist* admits the same in a paper *Generation Jobless* (April 27th 2013) while stressing that the classical economic opinions about the neutrality of technological advancement with regard to unemployment turned out to be simply false. On the other hand, however, the same weekly, in many other papers, points out that excessive employment and importance of labour unions are typical signs of faulty management of enterprises. Therefore, there is no doubt that *the combination of high technology and capitalist system results in fast automation and growing unemployment.*

This aspect of the impact of the informational revolution on the capitalist economy is particularly dangerous, since—as it is known from the pre-Keynesian work by Michał Kalecki, (see, e.g., Kalecki 1935)—economic demand is decisive for economic growth, but the megatrend of labour costs minimization results in a decrease of global demand. *For what money will people buy products in a society of almost full automation?*

The stratification related to this megatrend is expressed by fast growing income of the upper 1 % of the society—and this upper class invests the surplus earnings in so called virtual economy, in speculations on stock exchange and currency exchange. However, it is known since Hyman Minsky's *financial instability hypothesis* (Minsky 1974) that excessive stock exchange investments result in investment bubbles and following crises; thus, virtual economy, stimulated by high technology use, contributes to the instability of capitalism.

This is not the only one example of corruption of the capitalist system by high technology brought by the informational revolution. In the former chapter, it was mentioned that informational revolution contributed to the crisis of 2007–2010 by deepening the information asymmetry on financial markets. A much deeper analysis of the use of high technology by banks in order to exploit their clients (e.g., by automating the decisions about loan defaults, which enabled the banks to take over mortgages assets) is presented by Stiglitz (2012) in *The Price of Inequality*. Stiglitz describes many other examples of corruption of the capitalist system with the use of new technology.

It was also mentioned that the informational revolution (actually, its megatrend of digital integration) results in a large increase of the role of media, strengthening of diverse aspects of *the society of spectacle* (Debord 1967), and especially of the impact of multimedia advertisement on society. Since the advertiser obviously highlights only the positive aspects of advertised products, the proliferation of commercials results in the growth of informational asymmetry on the market. All people see this, but not all understand the fact that a multimedia advertisement influences the subconscious (or unconscious) much stronger than a verbal message. This in turn results from the fact that the immanent perception of humans (by all senses) processes several-hundred times bigger streams of information than textual or verbal perception.[1] Because of the strength of the multimedia influence, it is necessary to legally regulate the methods of advertisement in a much stricter way, e.g., empower the consumer protection offices even to penalize all commercials that misinform the consumers.

The growing influence of advertisers on media threatens also democracy, and results in a medial auto-censure. The owner or media editor limits such messages in medial transmission that might not suit the advertisers, hence might have a negative impact on the income from commercials. The results of such auto-censure are universally seen in the current media: the tone of the comments of a journal or a television channel is fully predictable. Other threats for democracy will be discussed in more detail in the end of this chapter.

The universality and power of multimedia information, the integration of television with the Internet and mobile telephony, result also in a specific effect deepening the awareness of stratification or economic exclusion. Today, a large part of global human population is affected by socio-economic exclusion, for diverse reasons—such as the migration of rural population to slums in megacities; or in Poland (among others), the too hasty, ill-conceived decision to liquidate the old state collective farms without any alternative for people employed there; or the difficulties in finding work for the new generations of youth. And the share of people excluded in human population will grow, unless we limit the ruthless use of new technology by the capitalist system. At the same time, the universality of multimedia information (and commercials) will clearly demonstrate to socially excluded inhabitants of slums in megacities of Africa or South America, or also to the inhabitants of godforsaken villages of old state collective farms, what is the standard of living of the richest people in the world. This will inevitably result in envy and rebellion, as discussed in more detail in Chap. 6.

---

[1]The power of human intuition results also from this fact; intuition separated from verbal and logical reasoning together with the development of language, see the evolutionary rational theory of intuition in (Wierzbicki 2015).

The next essential aspect of the corruption of classic market mechanisms caused by the impact of the informational revolution is the *oligopolization of high technology markets* mentioned in Chap. 2. This is combined with the *megatrend of reduction of marginal production costs in knowledge-based production*: if knowledge becomes the essential productive factor, then the cost of production of a next item becomes marginally low. This trend is stressed by Rifkin (2014) in his futurologist work *The Zero Marginal Cost Society*. However, he does not acknowledge that this trend was earlier and deeper analyzed in Kameoka and Wierzbicki (2005), see also Wierzbicki (2015). Rifkin maintains that the trend in consideration will bring to an end the capitalism such as we know today, not noticing how the contemporary capitalism defends itself against this trend precisely by oligopolization of high technology markets with tacit price fixing.

A deeper analysis of this phenomenon can be twofold. One way is to recall the work of Sylos (1962) who has shown that prices on oligopoly markets do not have any relation to marginal production costs and are set by the leader or leaders of the market in a way to cover full production costs with an arbitrarily defined profit—but low enough to prevent new entries to the market. Another is based on an application of the classical game theory assuming competitive markets in a situation of oligopoly. If a market operates in conditions of free price competition, but the number of market players is limited for any sort of reasons, then using the game theory we can prove that the price determined by competitive behaviour will amount to:

$$p_i = m_{pc}\, \varepsilon / (\varepsilon - y_i) \qquad (3.1)$$

where m_{pc} are marginal production costs, ε is the elasticity of demand with respect to price (close or even greater than 1 for products of fundamental importance, such as pharmaceuticals or telecommunication services), while y_i is the market share of the *i*th producer on the market (if consumers are accustomed to the products of a given producer, then the prices on an oligopolistic markets need not be equalized; thus, p_i is the price charged by the *i*th producer).

If the market shares are very small, $y_i \to 0$, then obviously the price on an ideal market amounts to $p = m_{pc}$. If there are five producers on the market, e.g. five pharmaceutical companies offering a given type of medical pills, and they have equal market shares $y_i = 0, 2$ at $\varepsilon = 1$, then the competitive price would be only 25 % higher than marginal production costs. However, in the current market situation the marginal production costs (e.g., the cost of producing an additional pill of a given medical product) on high-tech markets are ridiculous small, *and the actual prices charged today are many times (sometimes over a hundred times) higher than those resulting from free competition.*

This is possible on oligopolistic market, as observed already by Sylos Labini, due to a *tacit price fixing*: all producers analyze what prices are typical of a given market, and subsequently maintain in unison that their prices must cover high costs of new technology; they apply comparable prices by no means resulting from market competition. The high profits resulting from such dealings obviously motivate other market players to enter such markets, but the initial costs of knowledge about new technologies result in massive barriers to market entry, hence the number of market players on high technology markets remains limited, chances of small enterprises to get there are small and at most they become subcontractors of the main market players. Most countries have, admittedly, anticartel regulations preventing *open price fixing* (a cartel is a group of producers that openly agrees to apply a given market price). But it is very difficult to detect *tacit price fixing*: the actual prices of new technologies are internal information of producers who also try not to disclose to regulatory authorities the data concerning actual marginal production costs.

Worse still, new digital technologies result in the emergence of new monopolies; there are many such examples (Google, Amazon, etc.). The neoliberal economics maintains that new technologies result in a destruction of old monopolies on the market without state intervention, but this is another example of propaganda defending the neoliberal slogan that the market is always correct.[2] That actually the reverse is true, that new technologies create new monopolies, was recently admitted by *The Economist* in an editorial *Should governments break up digital monopolies?* (November 27 2014), even if this editorial paper shows also a neoliberal tendency by not quite convincing arguments defending these monopolies.

Therefore, the contemporary capitalism defends itself against the megatrend of reduction of marginal production costs, which is not noticed by Jeremy Rifkin, by oligopolization of high technology markets with tacit price fixing, or even formation of new monopolies. This of course enables a ruthless exploitation of consumers, especially on the markets of such fundamental products as medicines. Therefore, we should not believe that the megatrend of reduction of marginal production costs alone will result in the end of capitalism as we know it today. Eventually, it might lead at most (slowly, because paradigmatic theories are durable) economists to finally notice how their tales about the free market miss the reality of high technology markets with strongly decreasing marginal production costs, and will modify their theories, accepting the results of Sylos Labini. Therefore, it is difficult to perceive a mechanism that will result in a spontaneous modification of capitalism due to diminishing marginal costs.—Jeremy Rifkin suggests that spontaneous *collaborative commons* will serve as such mechanism, but it is doubtful that this will really work.

We should thus search for another solution: allow the capitalists to obtain high profits (if they are most talented and entrepreneurial), but *change the taxation system in such a way so that taxes are lower when entrepreneurs provide working places for people, and much higher, if they use only automated work*. Such taxation alone might be not sufficient and other solutions might be also necessary, such as the *citizen pension* suggested by Standing (2011), *shortening of working time, strengthening of public sector,* see Chap. 7. However, such taxation might

---

[2]Both Stiglitz (2012), and in Poland Woś, in his new book *Dziecięca choroba liberalizmu (The Infant Disease of Liberalism* 2014) present many examples of such false neoliberal slogans serving to convince the society that the market and entrepreneurs should be left alone.

help capitalists *to better realize, in their own interest, their main social duty: to provide working places for people,* and it might *harness precisely those who are most talented and entrepreneurial to invent new professions and jobs.*

Such solutions will be discussed in more detail in Chap. 7, here it must be stressed only that they will encounter an obvious resistance from the majority of capitalists, media and traditional economists, hence they can be introduced only under a strong, general democratic pressure, with a sufficient impact of the most poor and excluded layers. Therefore, I will devote the rest of this chapter to the impact of the informational revolution on democracy.

This impact is a subject of large controversy. On the one hand, the first generation of creators and users of the Internet, starting with the creators of computer networks—say, Baran (1960)—believed that computer networks and the Internet will strengthen democracy, providing an universal and cheap access to information; the universality of cheap access is still the main motivation of most creators of informational technologies. On the other hand, large media enterprises, using the slogans of intellectual property rights, went as far as to order special software tools called hypocritically *DRM (Digital Rights Management)*, actually serving to limit the access to and use of digital content of network resources. There are many such tools used to limit the access to films, television, documents etc.; they might have the form of special codes, so-called watermarks, metadata, etc. DRM solutions encountered sharp critique of diverse communities. This critique is best expressed by the opinion of Richard Stallman that it is a malicious addition to a code, a feature designed to disadvantage the user of that code, hence an attribute that cannot be tolerated.[3] This is only an example of the ferocious fight for the freedom of access to information on the Internet.

Outside of the Internet, there are many attacks on the concept or value of democracy, particularly from the right-wing. The informational revolution enables a broadening of direct democracy, network voting on diverse issues; some politicians are afraid that direct democracy would limit their role. The informational revolution has an obvious consequence that specialists in information technologies get about more easily in the world of the Internet and have better employment chances; right-wing sociologists interpret this phenomenon as a sign of *netocracy*, a breakdown of democracy towards layered social structure, see e.g. (Bard and Söderqvist 2002). Attacks on democracy are quite diverse, but all express the unwillingness to accept the right to vote of the poorest and excluded layers of society. On the other hand, left wing papers proclaiming "the end of democracy" (e.g., Hamm 2014) are limited to a correct but superficial statement that the strong growth of inequality in the current world results in the concentration of actual power in the richest layer of society.

What is then the actual value of democracy in times after the informational revolution? An answer might be based on an additional conclusion derived from meta-ethical premises discussed in Chap. 2. Since next generations will be faced

---

[3]See http://www.gnu.org/philosophy/right-to-read.html.

with new threats and crises, also those resulting from the informational revolution, hence—as recognised already by Rawls (1971)—we should leave them a most just social system. But the arguments of Rawls might be strengthened: *a diversity of opinions provides a greater systemic robustness*, in the face of a crisis it is better to have the possibility of listening to many opinions—and even if we can expect that "a perspective is determined by the point of sitting", nevertheless the opinions of the poorest and the middle class will be less influenced by the "point of sitting" than the opinions of the richest. Actually, the arguments of Baran (1960), who proposed a dispersion of information in a network in order to increase its robustness, were similar—moreover, he proved a greater robustness of such solution by computer simulation. Therefore, *democracy is a systemic backup that provides a greater robustness of a social system in the face of inevitable crises that will be brought yet by the informational revolution*. Democracy is not an ideal system, as noted by Churchill (in *The Second World War* 1948–1953), except that it is best between known systems.

We should add that between the critics of democracy there are also opinions that refer to the efficiency of the centralist "state capitalism" in China observed today—even if actually the Chinese system is a specific hybrid of Chinese tradition of central government, a socialist mono-party system with a specific variation of the slogan of "internal party democracy", and finally—market economy combined with central planning (all according to the Chinese philosophy of the unity of contradictions). This hybrid is rather efficient and for cultural reasons might be rather durable, but only provided that the opinions of social masses will be listened to (e.g., in relation to fighting corruption), hence democratic principles will also be used.

Therefore, it is important, as written by Pietro Speroni di Fenizio in *Ethical Technology*[4] under the headline „The Future of Democracy", that "*people of the 21st century do not believe politicians, but want to take part more directly both in legislature and in political decisions*". While this does not mean full direct democracy yet, nevertheless it does mean its gradual increase due to the advancement of information technology tools serving democracy. Such tools are, e.g., appropriate systems of gathering public opinions, such as the system MixedInk (used, among others, by president Barack Obama for analyzing public opinions). The informational revolution can supply tools strengthening democracy, but what is important is their appropriate use.

References

Babbage, Ch. (1835). *On the economy of machinery and manufactures* (4th ed.). London: Charles Knight.
Baran, P. (1960). Reliable digital communications systems using unreliable network repeater nodes. *RAND Corporation papers, document P-995*.Retrieved 29 March, 2011 from http://www.rand.org/pubs/papers/P1995.html.

---

[4]http://ieet.org/index.php/IEET/more/speroni20120427.

Bard, A., & Söderqvist, J. (2002). *Netocracy—the new power elite and life after capitalism*. UK: Reuters/Pearsall.

Churchill, W. (1948–1953). *The second world war*. Boston: Houghton Mifflin.

Debord, G. (1967). *The society of the spectacle*. London: Black & Red. (English translation in 1970; rev. ed. 1977).

Hamm, B. (2014) The end of democracy as we know it. *Information Clearing House,* http://www.informationclearinghouse.info/article38441.htm.

Kalecki, M. (1935). A macrodynamic theory of business cycles. *Econometrica, 3*, 327–344.

Kameoka, A., & Wierzbicki, A. P. (2005). *A vision of new era of knowledge civilization*. Kobe: 1th World Congress of IFSR.

Minsky, H. P. (1974). The modeling of financial instability: An introduction. *Modeling and Simulation. Proceedings of the Fifth Annual Pittsburgh Conference* 5.

Rawls, J. (1971). *A theory of justice*. Cambridge: Belknap Press.

Rifkin, J. (2014). *The zero marginal cost society: The internet of things, the collaborative commons and the eclipse of capitalism*. New York: Palgrave Macmillan Trade.

Standing, G. (2011). *The precariat. The new dangerous class*. London, New York: Bloomsbury Academic.

Stiglitz, J. (2012). *The price of inequality: How today's divided society endangers our future*. New York: Norton & Co.

Sylos, Labini P. (1962). *Oligopoly and technical progress*. Cambridge: Harvard University Press.

The Economist. (2013). Generation jobless: The global rise of youth unemployment. (April 27th, 2013).

The Economist. (2014). Should governments break up digital monopolies? (November 27th, 2014).

Wierzbicki, A. P. (2015). *Techne$_n$: Elements of recemt history of information technologies with epistemological conclusions*. Heidelberg: Springer.

Woś, R. (2014). *Dziecięca choroba liberalizmu*. Warszawa: Studio Emka. (in Polish, The Infant Disease of Liberalism).

Chapter 4
End of Communism and a Beginning of the End of Capitalism

Abstract This chapter presents the opinion that the end of communism was related to the destruction of proletariat due to two factors: globalisation and automation, but forthcoming automation and robotisation will also contribute to the end of capitalism. A review of opinions of authors writing about the end of capitalism is presented, but opinions about precise factors and ways of such end are rare among them. Most incisive opinions postulate that capitalism will be replaced by some hybrid of capitalism and socialism, but do not specify in what way this will occur. The author concludes that a serious threat to capitalism is a gradual increase of the number and importance of *precariat*, a layer of people usually young, relatively well educated, but without steady work and hope of a stable situation in life. It will be precariat who will either start a revolution, or force capitalism to reform itself essentially.

Keywords End of communism · End of capitalism · Threats to capitalism · What will replace capitalism · How capitalism will be replaced · Importance of precariat

Before we proceed to further analysis of the megatrend of minimization of the costs of labour, it is worthwhile to present a slightly different view than the popular opinion on the history of the last 40 years, together with the fall of communism or rather of the block of the countries of the so-called real socialism, and in particular those aspects of this history that launched this megatrend, followed by a discussion of diverse opinions on the end of capitalism.

In 1980 Alvin Toffler, in his book *The Third Wave*, formulated a prognosis that the progress of information technology will lead to the end of importance and to the destruction of industrial proletariat, as well as to the emergence of an informational society that can develop, however, only in a democratic and market system. While I disagree with Toffler as to the numbering of civilization eras (there were many more than three), nevertheless I consider his prognosis as exceptionally incisive and important: it was actually *a carefully formulated prognosis of the end of*

© The Author(s) 2016
A.P. Wierzbicki, *The Future of Work in Information Society*,
SpringerBriefs in Economics, DOI 10.1007/978-3-319-33909-2_4

the system of real socialism. Thus, the neoliberal opinion of Taleb (2007), that the fall of communism was an example of the *black swan phenomenon* that nobody predicted, was simply false.

What is more important, the Toffler's prognosis was known to president Ronald Reagan (who apparently did not read the Toffler's book, but the opinions contained therein was presented to the him by his advisors). He was very satisfied with such prediction and took twofold actions.

Firstly—together with his ideological ally, prime minister Margaret Thatcher of the United Kingdom—he intensified measures started already earlier and leading to diminishing the role and to a destruction of industrial proletariat in the USA and in the United Kingdom. These measures were supported by a neoliberal economic ideology that became popular at that time and included support for the export of industrial work to less developed countries (investments transferring industrial production to other countries, offering lower costs of labour under the slogans of globalization), with a parallel attack on the role of labour unions. It is significant that the destruction of the importance of labour unions in the United Kingdom and in the USA occurred at the same time when these countries proclaimed (and actually implemented) the support for the labour union Solidarity in Poland.

The second kind of measures of Ronald Reagan concerned the use of high technology to weaken the system of the countries of real socialism. All these countries (not only Poland in the time of martial law) were already in a crisis ensuing from the lack of sufficient technological progress. This resulted from a weakness of the market system in those countries and the lack of a positive feedback between technological progress and the market, characteristic of a developed market economy (see Wierzbicki 2015). Thus, the American president started to intensify armaments based on high technology, the so-called star wars, in order to increase the pressure on the block of real socialist countries.

This weakness of the non-market system of research and development was known to the intelligence services of the countries of this block that provided this information to the military and political authorities. I know this because in 1986, delegated by the Future Studies Committee of the Polish Academy of Sciences, I presented the predictions of Toffler at a meeting of the government of Poland headed by general Wojciech Jaruzelski. Some ministers of this government sharply criticized me for that, but the minister of defence, general Florian Siwicki, supported me and admitted that his intelligence service informed him about the superiority of the market system as regards the development of new technology. He was supported by the prime minister, general Wojciech Jaruzelski, who stated that he read the book of Toffler and that I correctly present the forecasts contained in that book. Possibly, the predictions of Toffler contributed to the peaceful systemic transformation of Poland in 1989.

Nevertheless, we should suspect that Poland was not an exception and the predictions of Toffler was known to other political leaders of the countries of the block of real socialism, in particular to Mikhail Gorbachev. It should be stressed that the current historiography imprecisely presents motivations of those political leaders. Many of them sincerely believed that they represent proletariat and a vision of the fall of its importance or of a conflict with a labour union representing it was a personal tragedy for them (in the introductory chapter, I quoted a private opinion on this issue offered to me much earlier by Adam Rapacki).

Less informed about forthcoming changes was the proletariat itself. In the USA or in the United Kingdom, these changes meant a destruction and impoverishment of industrial proletariat, and contributed to the neoliberal theses about the end of proletariat, emergence of a class-less society and the end of history (see, e.g., Fukuyama 1992). Such theses are evidently false, since the concept of proletariat denotes not only the industrial proletariat but also all low-paid working class, including the unemployed, and today also precariat (see, e.g., Standing 2011). However, the industrial proletariat becomes actually destructed because of the megatrends of dematerialization of work and minimization of its costs—either by globalization, or later—automation. The labour union Solidarity in Poland was not informed of this by its advisors, particularly by neoliberal economists.

The victory of Solidarity in 1989 in Poland brought, on the one hand, excellent general results: democracy, better market supply, average growth of income, and later—accession to the European Union. On the other hand, however, the average growth of income meant actual stratification, fast growth of the income of the richest and a drop of the income of the poorest, since the economic advisors of Solidarity applied to it—and to entire Poland—a shock therapy under an evidently false slogan that "there is no third way". It was sufficient to look over Baltic Sea, to Scandinavian countries with the best indexes of human development in the world, for an example of a third way; moreover, that slogan was a logical error already when it was formulated.[1]

The shock therapy included a destruction of industry in Poland, since the sale of state enterprises as a part of privatization programme usually resulted in their liquidation. The more advanced was a state enterprise in Poland, such as ELWRO in Wrocław or ship turbine plant in Elbląg, the faster it was liquidated by foreign capitalists buying it who had seen in Poland only a market for sales, and eliminated competition. Often, the shock therapy used also opinions of international consulting companies who did not hide the fact that they advise according to their own interests. Thus, Solidarity was actually abandoned as a worn out tool by its advisors, see also (Kuroń 2004).

Even if the introduction of market economy in Poland brought an improvement of market supply and average improvement of income of population, it brought also a substantial increase of inequality, loss of income by the poorest, increase of unemployment and social exclusion, and finally the emergence of precariat, discussed in the next chapter. Even if the introduction of a democratic system

---

[1]This logical error is related to the fact that precisely in 1991 Zdzisław Pawlak published an English version of his book (Pawlak 1991) on the applications of tertiary logic; he noted that *there is always a third way in large data sets* (for each logical sentence there might be many data confirming it, many data contradicting it, but there are also many data neither confirming nor contradicting it). See Wierzbicki (2015) on the issue of *logical pluralism.*

essentially increased the scope of individual freedom, media still use auto-censure and propagate "politically correct" opinions. *I write this book in the hope that we succeed in avoiding a revolutionary way of transforming capitalism—but I see the danger of such a way and the need of a transformation.*

The ways and symptoms of the *megatrend of minimization of the costs of work* and the destruction of industrial proletariat related to it in the world are diverse. In less developed countries to which the industry from more developed countries is exported (and in China which can hardly be called a less developed country today), industrial proletariat increases its importance, is better paid, and contributes to the global increase of the middle class. Moreover, neoliberal economists maintain that there is no problem—industrial proletariat might find work in services. But these are transitory phenomena: if the cost of work can be diminished by automation and robotization, capitalism will use this possibility also in less developed countries (and also in China as well as in services where robots can work in future). If the income of the richest 1 % of population in the USA grows over three times faster than the global GDP (and the global GDP grows faster than the GDP in the USA) due to the minimization of the costs of work, this indicates a loss of income and an actual stratification of the middle class.[2] A part of middle class in the USA, specialists in information technologies, earns better—but a large part of it earns less, which contributes to growing income inequalities. If such phenomena occur in the USA, they can also occur in future in the rest of the world.

Moreover, *The Economist* (issue April 21 2012) clearly urges British capitalists to use the new possibilities of a *third industrial revolution* (considering electrification as the second one). This slogan expresses the possibility of building fully automated factories, practically devoid of workers except a few specialists supervising automats and robots. *The Economist* advances this slogan and tries to convince British capitalists to invest in such factories because it would restore industrial primacy of the United Kingdom. However, the journal does not recognise that together with this slogan, it promotes also *the beginning of an end of capitalism* that today is based on a mass social economic demand—and for what money such demand will exist, if all production is automated? *Therefore, megatrend of minimization of the costs of work leads, in a further perspective, to the end of capitalism such as we know it today.*

The slogan of *the end of capitalism* is not new and not necessarily related to socialist movement. During last decades, it was many times discussed from diverse viewpoints.

Drucker (1993) writes about a *post-capitalist society;* he substantiates this term by referring to the transformation of capitalism resulting from the knowledge-based production (he also uses the term *knowledge society*—which contributed

---

[2]If the income of the richest part of population is growing faster than the GDP, then it must be so at the cost of remaining, poorer part of population whose income must grow slower or even fall. Moreover, because a large part of the growth of the GDP is eaten by inflation; hence net of inflation the income of the poorest part of population certainly decreases.

to the discussions of *knowledge-based economy*). He also draws attention to the separation of capitalist property from the traditional family property (the latter had a positive impact because of the care of a company's reputation). Both these observations, even if justified, do not include the effects of the megatrend of minimizing the costs of work that will change capitalism more essentially.

Wallerstein (1999) writes more fundamentally about *the end of the world that we know;* he also predicts that an end of capitalism will occur in several dozen years—not in a revolutionary way, but for diverse reasons, to which he includes: a diminishing reservoir of cheap labour (formerly coming from agricultural regions); a democratisation of society (together with expectations of a fair remuneration for work, provision for old age, access to suitable health care, and education of children); a crisis of state; and the pollution of environment. However, he does not notice a more fundamental reason: the destruction of the socio-economic demand as the foundation of capitalism if the current megatrend of minimization of the cost of work is upheld in a further perspective. Neither he notes that *we shall soon face the choice: either we will reform capitalism in a democratic way in order to contain the megatrend of minimization of the cost of work, or we will be confronted by a global revolution.*

Greenwald (2013) poses a question whether capitalism is really dying, but he answers negatively (to no surprise, since he is a Wall Street expert), stressing only that variants of capitalism avoiding excessive inequality, such as in Scandinavia, result in a much better quality of life. On the other hand, Rifkin (2014) believes in the end of capitalism, but uses and imprecise term "*the zero marginal cost revolution*" without acknowledging how contemporary capitalism actually defends itself against this danger by using tacit price fixing on oligopolistic markets.

The webpage *The End of Capitalism* presents diverse opinions related to the headline slogan that is becoming increasingly important after the financial-economic crisis 2007–2010, but all these opinions document a growing insecurity and a sense of possible danger, a condensation of revolutionary air. A rather popular opinion is that capitalism cannot be repaired and should be replaced by something—but by what and in what a way? Richard Koch[3] says that "the end of industry means the end of capitalism". Harvey (2014) focuses on contradictions of capitalism (seventeen in number, while not hiding a Marxist way of analysis) and substantiates with them the opinion that capitalism is passing away—but he does not define the way it shall end and writes only about "the hope of revolutionary humanism". Only Streeck (2014) asks the question how capitalism will end, and sees this end as deepening dysfunctionalities of capitalism, worsening indexes of economic growth, financial stability, social equality etc.; thus, he sees the end of capitalism as a process, not an event. Nevertheless, he uses a telling expression "plutocrats and plunder". All these opinions indicate a gradual growth of a critical mood towards capitalism.

---

[3]http://www.huffingtonpost.com/richard-koch/the-end-of-capitalism_b_4593969.html.

In the paper *Towards the End of Capitalism* (2006), Rafi Moor[4] presents what is perhaps the most incisive opinion on the possibilities of the end of capitalism. He distinguishes capitalism and socialism as not only two social systems, but also two opposite ideologies: capitalism stresses the right of an individual to fight for his own interests, socialism stresses common interests and the necessity to limit competition between individuals. Personally, I formulate it more bluntly: *capitalism is based on human greed, socialism believes in more noble motivations*—but this is precisely the advantage of capitalism. Moor notes this also by stating that socialism has fallen because its ideas were too good to be realized by people. He asks also the question whether capitalism is ethical—and answers that not quite, that ethics should limit capitalism. To the further question, whether capitalism is efficient, he also answers negatively, questioning the opinions of neoliberal economists in that respect. He maintains that capitalism is efficient only with reference to such values that are easily transformed to money, but is not efficient as regards more general values, such as the quality of environment or the quality of life; these require a social agreement and monitoring of the functioning of capitalism.

Moor concludes that capitalism is an unbalanced and unstable system (even if it turned out to be more robust than socialism), hence must be modified. He does not believe that a revolutionary way is real today, but he notices the frustration and disappointment of poorest layers of society and diverse social movements critical to capitalism: alter-globalists, ecological movements, green parties. He does not notice, however, the connection between the problems of the end of work and of capitalism, nor the impact of neo-Thatcherism, an ideology promoting self-employment as a response to the problems of the end of work, but actually accelerating the end of capitalism. Nevertheless, Moor asks with what we could replace capitalism and responds that surely not by socialism, only by some hybrid of capitalism and socialism. He does not specify what hybrid it will be, nor when it should occur—he concludes only (and I believe, correctly) that it will happen in the current, 21st century.

Both the perception of the growing critical or even revolutionary feelings and serious discussions about the end of capitalism persuaded me to write this book. Even if the growing revolutionary feelings might be only a transient fashion, nevertheless I believe that the serious threat for capitalism is gradual increase of the number and importance of *precariat*, a layer of people usually young, relatively well educated, but without steady work and hope of a stable situation in life. Various aspects of the growth of precariat will be discussed in the next chapter, here I discuss only the prognosis of its growth rate. Urbański (2014) maintains that today, precariat makes up circa 60 % of the global labour force; it is probably a correct estimate, if we use a broad concept of precariat. However, if we limit it to well-educated but not permanently employed labour force, today mostly young, we could estimate its share at about 20 % of global labour force. However, this share will be systematically growing, with a rate of circa 5–8 % per decade. In 50 years, it might become a decisive force—and it will be precariat (see also Kleiber et al. 2011) who will start a revolution, or force capitalism to reform itself essentially.

---

[4]http://www.rafimoor.com/english/TEOCE.htm.

References

Drucker, P. F. (1993). *Post-capitalist society*. New York: HarperBusiness.

Fukuyama, F. (1992). *The end of history and the last man*. New York: Free Press, Macmillan Inc.

Greenwald, I. (2013). Is capitalism dying? *Wall Street Journal, 1*(07), 2013.

Harvey, D. (2014). *Seventeen contradictions and the end of capitalism*. Oxford: Oxford University Press.

Kleiber, M., Kleer, J., Wierzbicki, A. P., Galwas, B., Kuźnicki, L., & Sadowski, Z., et al. (2011). *Report Poland 2050. Committee of Future Studies at the Presidium of P.Ac.Sc.* Warsaw.

Kuroń, J. J. (2004). *Rzeczpospolita dla moich wnuków (in Polish, The Republic for my Grandchildren)*. Warszawa: Wydawnictwo Rosner i Wspólnicy.

Pawlak, Z. (1991). *Rough sets—theoretical aspects of reasoning about Data*. Dordrecht: Kluwer.

Rifkin, J. (2014). *The zero marginal cost society: The internet of things, the collaborative commons and the eclipse of capitalism*. New York: Palgrave Macmillan Trade.

Standing, G. (2011). *The precariat. The new dangerous class*. London/New York: Bloomsbury Academic.

Streeck, W. (2014). How will capitalism end? *New Left Review*. (May–June 2014).

Taleb, N. N. (2007). *The black swan: The impact of the highly improbable*. New York: Random House.

The Economist. (2012). A third industrial revolution. (April 21, 2012).

Urbański, J. (2014). *Prekariat i nowa walka klas (in Polish, Precariat and New Class Struggle)*. Warszawa: Instytut Wydawniczy Książka i Prasa.

Wallerstein, I. (1999). *The end of the world as we know it: Social science for the twenty-first century*. Minneapolis: University of Minnesota Press.

Wierzbicki, A. P. (2015). *Techne_n: Elements of recent history of information technologies with epistemological conclusions*. Heidelberg: Springer.

Chapter 5
A Vision of the End of Work and the Emergence of Precariat

Abstract This Chapter discusses the concept of *the end of work* and its increasing importance as a threat to capitalism because of the acceleration of replacement of labour by capital due to positive feedback. A review of opinions of authors writing about the future of work is given. Many specialists do not believe in the end of work, but the inventing of new professions and new workplaces is simply too slow today to counterbalance the megatrend of minimisation of costs of work due to the replacement of labour by capital. Future society cannot effectively function without market; but market society without work might be perceived today as a society of large and deep stratification, with the majority of people in social exclusion. Most excluded layer will be precariat, hence factors leading to the emergence and growth of precariat are discussed in detail. An additional factor is the megatrend of improving average education, hence it will be the educated precariat that will enforce future changes of capitalism. This will occur either in a revolutionary way, or in the way of rather essential modifications of the assumptions of capitalism if it could be achieved by democratic reforms.

Keywords End of work · Social stratification and exclusion · Precariat · Megatrend of improving average education · Future changes of capitalism · Revolution or democratic reforms

The concept of *the end of work* was introduced (1995) by Jeremy Rifkin in his futuristic book *The End of Work*. Rifkin predicted correctly that technological progress, automation and advance of robotics will lead to the end of work, even if he did not analyzed more deeply the mechanisms of contemporary capitalism that accelerate this end. The vision of Jeremy Rifkin was many times criticized, sometimes even ridiculed—but it was only a vision, and one insufficiently substantiated. The critics of the concept of *the end of work* simply would not believe in it, since—as already mentioned in Chap. 3—the classical economics maintained that technological progress cannot result in the increase of unemployment. Indeed, but it is a theory that concerned times before the informational revolution, and the latter gives to capitalists many new tools to minimize the cost of work—and

A.P. Wierzbicki, *The Future of Work in Information Society*,
SpringerBriefs in Economics, DOI 10.1007/978-3-319-33909-2_5

capitalists obviously use these tools eagerly. Some economists would say that since the beginnings of industrial revolution capital has replaced labour—indeed, but today this happens on an unprecedented scale and at an unprecedented pace. Therefore, I call it *a megatrend of minimization of the costs of work*; and indeed, in a further perspective it will lead to the end of work as we know today.

Earlier, similar opinion was expressed by Adam Schaff in his works for the Club of Rome (see Friedrichs and Schaff 1982; also Schaff 1997). He maintained that work will be dying as a result of a new scientific-technological revolution, that in 20–30 years the proletariat will disappear, which in turn will cause also the class of capitalists to disappear. He did not explain, however, in what way will it happen. He recognised that work is necessary for psychological and social reasons. Such importance of work for self-fulfilment of people was stressed also by Bogdan Suchodolski in his works for the Future Studies Committee of PAS (e.g., Suchodolski 1984). An open question remains as to whether the neoliberal variant of the contemporary capitalism creates conditions for assuring such self-fulfilment?

An incisive analysis of these issues is presented in the chapter *Nowy świat pracy* (*New World of Work*) by Zofia Jacukowicz in the book (Borkowska 2004). Jacukowicz stresses that the opinion about dying work is by no means universally accepted, and in many countries there are serious disputes how to limit unemployment through creating new working places. However, I personally believe that such measures will not bring sufficient effects if capitalist are not sufficiently motivated to an actual, not only slogan-like creation of new working places. Jacukowicz expresses also the opinion that the extent of work will be growing because of the needs of development of less rich countries and their attempts to keep up with more rich countries. Personally, I consider this to be correct, but it is only a transitory effect. Already today we observe in less rich countries similar phenomena as in the richest ones; for example, the emergence of precariat and social issues related to that phenomenon, discussed in more detail in the end of this chapter—and in the next 50 years the problems related to the end of work will be growing also in the less rich countries.

The share of people employed in production activities in industry and agriculture in developed countries decreased more than twice in the last 40 years (to less than 30 %, much less in the USA). Therefore, many sociologists and economists accepted the thesis about *service society*, maintaining that remaining people will find work in services. Today, however, because of the development of network services on the Internet and the perspective of service work being replaced by robots, the service society turns out to be transitory: the offers of service work begin to diminish due to the increase of network services, and the first applications of robots in supermarkets emerge. We should expect, therefore, that any reasons for divagations about service society will disappear during next 50 years.

The question what will happen, if we will be replaced in work by automatons and robots, was discussed many times even earlier (e.g. by Lem 1961). A superficial answer is optimistic: fine, people are lazy by nature, we will have time for relaxation, entertainment, games (*homo ludens* will replace *homo faber*).

However, after a deeper reflection a question comes: fine, but what will be the source of income of people without work? Again, a superficial answer is: obviously, money. However, money is only an equivalent of goods and services that people (or their families) supplied to society and expect reciprocity, "there is no bread without money". Therefore, perhaps we should extinguish also money and the market and organize a class-less egalitarian society according to the known principle "to everybody according to their needs"? This would be possible, because in the far future (not so far—personally I think that after a fifty, at most one hundred fifty years) automatons and robots will replace us completely in every production branch—industrial, agricultural, mining—and also in services?

Fine, but other questions arise (not taken up, e.g., by Rifkin writing about a post-market society): how to organize a distribution of goods, products and services in such society, who will decide whether the needs of people are truly justified (everybody might want to have, e.g., an allotment on the Moon)? Even if such society would really function (our East-European experiences with the so-called real socialism indicate that most probably it would not), how and in what way shall we arrive at such a society from the current version of capitalism?

Thus, we cannot imagine an efficiently functioning society without money and market. This is confirmed by the experience of China that could not function efficiently before market reforms. And this, in turn, suggests that the vision of the end of work is not optimistic, is rather dangerous.

What would money mean in a market society without work? Money will belong to owners of productive and service enterprises and to a small number of specialists necessary to supervise robots and automations working for these owners. Moreover, money will belong to rich people by inheritance. And what about the rest of society? Well, it will make a living out of unemployment benefits and old age pensions—which will actually mean social exclusion, if the current trends are upheld. Therefore, *market society without work might be perceived today as a society of large and deep stratification, with the majority of people in social exclusion.* Clearly, it is difficult to imagine that robots will replace people in all professions, such as, e.g., teachers and public administration, and judiciary—and therefore we should try to preserve extensive employment in the public sector, see also (Galwas 2014), but this will not provide work for the majority of people.

When writing about *the megatrend of dematerialisation of work* (Wierzbicki 2000), I had the hope that people will invent new professions and places of work. Today, most of studies concerning the future of work is focused on this. Neoliberal economics maintains optimistically that entrepreneurs, using new technologies, will create new places of work. Hopes are concentrated on temporary work, networked work, on *crowdsourcing* (which means distributed group-wise networked work on the Internet using the abilities of a dispersed group of people and common tools in *clouds,* collections of software tools accessible by network and shared by users).

All such opinions, however, do not take into account the dynamics of the waves of social penetration of new technologies, related to the informational revolution. Still before this revolution, we lived through the wave of social penetration of *television*: the first ideas in 1878 (a Pole, Julian Ochorowicz) and 1880 (an American, George Carey), specific inventions of electronic camera and television receiver in 1922–28 (Vladimir Zworikin and Kalman Tihanyi, both emigrants from Eastern Europe to the USA), refinement and cheapening of such devices lasted until 1960, when in the USA the process of a social penetration of colour television begun, lasting until 1990. First in (1967), Guy Debord recognised worrying aspects of the social impact of television and formulated his thesis about *the spectacle society*. However, it was obviously already too late to influence in any way the wave of penetration of television, which developed in a sense inevitably, motivated by economic mechanisms and social demand.

The next waves developed similarly. I shall list first the three original waves of the informational revolution. *Electronic computers,* invented in 1931 by Vannevar Bush (analog computers) and in 1936 by Konrad Zuse (digital computers), started their social penetration in 1977 (personal computers, Apple 2 by Steve Jobs and Steve Wozniak); this process lasts until today and again, it is in a sense inevitable. Mobile *cellular telephony* was invented in 1943, but its social penetration started seriously only in 1990; the impact of this penetration, its effects on life and social customs today is enormous. Similarly *the Internet*: the initial idea in 1948 (again Vannevar Bush), the beginning of social penetration in 1992 (Timothy Berners-Lee), and the process of social penetration and integration with the other waves lasts until today.

And this is precisely the danger of new technologies: in the period of *delay* between the invention and the beginning of social penetration we speculate about possible effects, but nobody takes it seriously. Meanwhile, the initial inventions of the next three waves of the informational revolution have already occurred. *Robots* are universally used in industry, but they did not penetrate into universal social use in the form of human-like robots (they do not yet walk with us on the streets and in supermarkets, but they will, such as cellular phones do). *Knowledge engineering* (popularly called *artificial intelligence*, but this is an imprecise and misleading term) is not yet universally used; and similarly, *biomedical engineering*. These three waves have yet to start their social penetration and again it will be in a sense inevitable. However, the social penetration of *robots* and *knowledge engineering* will reinforce the megatrend of dematerialization of work, which together with maximization of profits will reinforce the megatrend of minimization of the costs of work.

All this will result in the end of work such as we know it today. I am not alone in such conclusions: the British consulting firm Deloitte published recently a report[1] warning that one third of British workplaces will be endangered due to the use of robots and computers. The firm concludes, however, that this will result in the increase of unemployment only among poorly educated people (I believe this conclusion to be not fully justified, since it does not take into account the megatrend of improvement of education, discussed in more detail later in this chapter).

---

[1]http://www.deloitte.com/view/en_GB/uk/ef762fa93fa89410VgnVCM1000003256f70aRCRD.htm.

What is necessary are rather more intensive *inventions of new professions and work,* which I hoped for when writing about the megatrends of the informational society (Wierzbicki 2000).

However today, while observing the disturbing trends of the growth of *precariat* discussed later in detail, I am coming to the conclusion that this *inventing of new professions is simply too slow.* People who should be responsible for inventing new professions and new workplaces, namely capitalists and plutocrats, are not motivated enough to take up this duty seriously. Even those plutocrats who are afraid of the results of contemporary trends of the development of capitalism (such as Nick Hanauer (2014) who fears that "The pitchforks are coming for us plutocrats") do not perceive that *their main duty should be an actual, not only slogan-like creation of new workplaces and professions.*

Meanwhile, the megatrends of dematerialization and minimization of the costs of work result in the growth of a new social layer, subclass or even a class of people called *precariat.* This layer emerged because of a concatenation of several factors. The first factor was the neoliberal slogan of *elastic labour market,* meaning really a limitation of the role of labour unions and modifications of labour legislation favourable for capitalists in such a way that they could employ people as they wish, on arbitrary conditions. I mentioned already in the Introduction that Stiglitz (2012) justly criticizes the opinion about a beneficial impact of elastic labour market on economy as a neoliberal myth, false and serving to conceal the real purpose: to give capitalists full freedom on the labour market. Precisely this freedom enabled the entrepreneurs to employ people—particularly younger— unsustainably, not only on short-term contracts, but also on the so-called *trash contracts,* most often with a possibility of firing at every moment without giving reasons. This obviously contributed to farther minimization of the costs of work. What is worse, the practices of elastic labour market—or, naming it correctly, of an arbitrary licence of employers in specifying the conditions of work—have soon penetrated into service work, e.g. the personnel of supermarkets, as well as to the so-called freelance professions that were traditionally accustomed to an elastic labour market, but even in this case employers exploited the possibility of determining arbitrary conditions of work.

The second factor was the possibility of minimizing the costs of work with the tools contributed by the informational revolution—computers, robots, etc. These tools make it possible to employ people disposable, temporary, elastic—and most efforts to counteract unemployment try to use such possibilities, but this only results in a growth of precariat.

The third factor of growth of precariat was globalization understood as a transfer of large industrial production from the richest countries to worse off ones that had a cheaper working force. In the most developed countries, this contributed directly to the loss of work of industrial proletariat that was forced to look for temporary employment. The growth of precariat in less developed countries was due to other factors, mostly through the elastic labour market, since in these countries labour legislation was not too strict and capitalists investing there demanded an elastic labour market, meaning the right to employ on the conditions suitable for the employer.

Finally, the fourth factor of precariat growth was the megatrend of universal improvement of education, because in my understanding the term precariat denotes well-educated people who are well prepared for work and diverse social roles, but cannot find lasting work as a result of ruthless labour market minimizing its costs, hence preferring precarious employment. My understanding of this term is close to that used in one of the first publications describing the emergence of precariat in Polish (Kleiber et al. 2011), but slightly different than used generally (Sowa 2010; Standing 2011; Urbański 2014) that defines precariat as all people employed unsustainably or unemployed, whatever their education level. Perhaps I should stress my understanding by using the term "well educated precariat", because *the issue of education is a crucial matter here that will decide about the role of precariat in the future.*

I am not concerned here with theoretical disputes whether precariat is a new class or only a new social layer, whether we have a class-less society (or post-class society, see Bauman 2000; for me, postmodernism was only a transitory intellectual fashion of the end of the 20th century, see Wierzbicki 2015), or whether proletariat remained but only changed, or whether laws of history exists (see Eagleton 2011). As regards the latter I believe that history in its details has highly accidental character, but nevertheless we can observe great civilization waves (see Braudel 1995) and great megatrends resulting from social inertia—either in the sense of demographic phenomena, or in the sense of slow adoption and penetration of new tools and technologies, or social customs. The slowness of changes related to such megatrends makes it possible to correctly predict future—obviously under the condition that such megatrends will be correctly identified and will not collapse soon.

A relatively good education of the youngest part of precariat results from a great global megatrend of betterment of education for all people in the world. In developed countries, this is related with the social realization of the fact that only appropriately educated young people have the chances of sound employment in the knowledge-based economy. This fact is universally understood, hence all families try to invest in the education of their children to prepare them best for future challenges. In Poland, it results in a large number of extra-mural, additional privately paid lessons for school pupils, as well as in a large share of privately paid courses at universities (not only private, also public ones).

This great *megatrend of improvement of average education* was documented in (Wierzbicki 2011). For example, in Finland the share of young people aged 20–24 years and attending university education exceeded 80 % already in 2000 and today it exceeds 90 %. These figures are much lower in Poland, since we started from a much lower level: the authorities in the period of the so-called real socialism were afraid of student revolts, hence they limited the share of young people at universities to 7 % administratively. After the democratisation of Poland, this share started to grow quickly, due to the awareness of Polish families that there are no chances of good employment either in Poland or abroad without university education—and due to the financial efforts of these families to secure university education for their children, using also a broad network of private tertiary schools.

Today, Poland holds the fifths place in the world concerning the percentage of university students in society (Banach 2011) and the index of young people aged 20–24 studying at universities exceeded 70 % already in 2008; we can forecast (Grzegorek 2011) that around 2050 it will exceed 95 %.

Because of a slow dynamics of demographic phenomena, the share of people with university education in the population of productive age changes much slower. Moreover, it is quite diversely interpreted. The so-called HRST index used by the OECD actually includes people without completed university education[2]; more precise data for Poland indicate that the index of people with completed university education can be much lower. On the other hand, the forecasts of dynamics of such indices can be quite precise, since they are based on long time sequences of data (Grzegorek 2011). The data indicates that this share has grown in the decade 2000–9 in Poland by about 9 % (from 25.3 to 34.1 % as for the HRST index, from 9.1 to 18.1 % as for the actual share of people with completed university education in Poland); this indicates a high educational effort of the Polish society. Even if it intensifies in the next decades, we can expect to arrive, around 2050, at the share of 60–70 % of university educated people at most. Obviously, a mass character of university education always results in a certain decrease of the quality of education, but nevertheless it contributes to an improvement of average education in a society.

This means, therefore, that young people in Poland, but also on average in the world, will be very well educated in 2050—and at the same time they will not have good perspectives of sustainable work, if the current megatrend of minimizing the costs of work will be upheld. This well-educated part of precariat (not necessarily young, because current precariat will age until that time) can be estimated given such assumption at 40–50 % of the global workforce in 2050; this means further accretion of revolutionary mood and, worse even, easiness of organization of revolutionary actions by educated precariat using the Internet.

Imagine a young man who graduated from a university and looks for work, but finds only temporary employment not corresponding to his education and aspirations. This results in postponing the time of starting a family and having children which obviously influences negatively demographic processes, but also causes frustration. Additionally, it is difficult to provide for a flat for himself and a possible partner in life, because banks give loans easily, but not for people without sustainable work and apartment. No wonder that either revolutionary or at least reformist moods will be dominating between precariat.

Such moods are already today quite popular between precariat, which is documented in detail in a book *Precariat and a New Class Struggle* (in Polish) by Jarosław Urbański. Urbański estimates rather highly (at 60–70 %) the share of current precariat in the global workforce. However, the problem is that current precariat is not yet very well educated on average, but this will gradually change,

---

[2]Not only people "having successfully completed an education at the third level", but also people who "are employed in an occupation where such an education is normally required", Canberra Manual, OECD 1995.

since the megatrend of improving education in the world is inevitable. This megatrend might collapse only by a totalitarian restriction of access to education of the poorest people, an improbable course of events in the current world. On the one hand, since unemployment is socially unpopular, governments support diverse forms of education as tools of fighting unemployment. On the other hand, electronic distant access to education through the Internet becomes very popular, including free education under the idea of *free access*.

All this substantiates the thesis that *it will be the educated precariat that will enforce future changes of capitalism*—in a revolutionary way, if it will not be given the possibility of democratic reforms (there are recently many publications on this topic, see e.g. Wielecki 2014), or in the way of rather essential modifications of the assumptions of capitalism, if such modifications can be achieved by way of democratic reforms. These two ways are described in the following two chapters.

References

Banach, C. Z. (2011). Strategia i kierunki reformy szkolnictwa wyższego w Polsce (in Polish, Strategy and directions of reform of university education in Poland). In J. Kleer, A. P. Wierzbicki, Z. Strzelecki & L. Kuźnicki (Eds.), *Wizja przyszłości Polski, Studia i analizy, Tom I Społeczeństwo i państwo* (In Polish, *A vision of the future of Poland, studies and analyses, Vol. I Society and state*). Warsaw: Committee for Future Studies at the Presidium of P.Ac.Sc.

Bauman, Z. (2000). *Liquid modernity*. Cambridge: Polity.

Borkowska, S. (Ed.). (2004). *Przyszłość pracy w XXI wieku (In Polish, The future of work in XXI century)*. Warsaw: IPiSS.

Braudel, F. (1995). *A history of civilizations*. London, New York: Penguin Books.

Debord, G. (1967) *The Society of the Spectacle*, (English translation in 1970; rev. ed. 1977) Black & Red, London.

Eagleton, T. (2011). *Why Marx was right*. Yale: Yale University Press.

Friedrichs, G., & Schaff, A. (1982). *Report to the club of Rome, microelectronics and society, for better and for worse*. Oxford: Pergamon Press.

Galwas, B. (2014). Świat po pierwszej dekadzie XXI wieku. Czas na państwo socjalne. (In Polish, The world after the first decade of XXI Century. The time for a social state). *Przyszłość—Świat, Europa, Polska* (pp. 64–86).

Grzegorek, J. (2011). Dane i projekcje statystyczne o rozwoju cywilizacyjnym Polski. (In Polish, Data and statistical projections concerning civilization development of Poland). In J. Kleer, A. P. Wierzbicki, Z. Strzelecki & L. Kuźnicki (Eds.), *Wizja Przyszłości Polski, Studia i analizy, Tom III Ekspertyzy*. (In Polish, *A vision of the future of Poland, studies and analyses, Vol. III Expert opinions*). Warsaw: Committee for Future Studies at the Presidium of P.Ac.Sc.

Hanauer, N. (2014) The Pitchforks are coming for US plutocrats. *POLITICOMAGAZINE*, July/August 2014.

Kleiber, M., Kleer, J., Wierzbicki, A. P., Galwas, B., Kuźnicki, L., Sadowski, Z., & Strzelecki, Z. (2011). *Report Poland 2050*. Warsaw: Committee for Future Studies at the Presidium of P.Ac.Sc.

Lem, St. (1961). *Powrót z Gwiazd*. Czytelnik, Warsaw. English translation *Return from the stars* (1980) Harcourt Brace.

Rifkin, J. (1995). *The end of work: The decline of the global labor force and the dawn of the post-market era*. Putnam Publishing Group.

Schaff, A. (1997). *Medytacje (In Polish, Meditations)*. Warsaw: Wydawnictwo Projekt.

Sowa, J. (2010). Prekariat—proletariat epoki globalizacji. *Robotnicy opuszczają miejsca pracy* (In Polish, The precariat—proletariat of the epoch of globalisation. *Workers leave workplaces*). Muzeum Sztuki, Łódź.

Standing, G. (2011). *The precariat. The new dangerous class*. London/New York: Bloomsbury Academic.

Stiglitz, J. (2012). *The price of inequality: How today's divided society endangers our future*. New York: Norton & Co.

Suchodolski, B. (1984). *Praca i samorealizacja, w Ewolucje polskiego systemu pracy (In Polish, Work and self-fulfilment, in evolutions of Polish system of work)*. Wrocław: Ossolineum.

Urbański, J. (2014). *Prekariat i nowa walka klas (In Polish, The precariat and a new class struggle)*. Warsaw: Instytut Wydawniczy Książka i Prasa.

Wielecki, K. (2014). Młodzi jeszcze podskoczą (In Polish, Youth will yet jump up). *Przegląd, 8–14*(09), 2014.

Wierzbicki, A. P. (2000). *Megatrends of information society and the emergence of knowledge science*. In *Proceedings of the International Conference on Virtual Environments for Advanced Modeling, JAIST, Tatsunokuchi Japan*.

Wierzbicki, A. P. (2011). Wizja i mechanizmy postępu w Polsce do 2050 roku (In Polish, A vision and mechanisms of progress until 2050). In J. Kleer, A. P. Wierzbicki, Z. Strzelecki & L. Kuźnicki (Eds.). *Wizja Przyszłości Polski, Studia i analizy, Tom I Społeczeństwo i państwo* (In Polish, *A vision of the future of Poland, studies and analyses, Vol. I Society and state*). Warsaw: Committee for Future Studies at the Presidium of P.Ac.Sc.

Wierzbicki, A. P. (2015). *Technen: Elements of recent history of information technologies with epistemological conclusions*. Heidelberg: Springer.

Chapter 6
A Possible Scenario of Annihilation

Abstract An exponential growth, an avalanche-like development observed in the last 300 years of the history of humanity is a result of positive feedbacks, and each such positive feedback process ends with encountering a constraint. Such constraint might be the end of work, if not alleviated by essential reforms. A revolutionary way of the change is extremely dangerous today, because of amassment of nuclear weapons and the spread of knowledge how to construct them. The chapter presents the dangers of the revolutionary way in a possible scenario of annihilation of human intelligence on Earth. Such scenario is exceptional, but similar scenarios become today not only possible, also even more probable.

Keywords Exponential growth · Avalanche-like development · Elastic labour market leading to a revolution · Dangers of a global revolution · Rarity of civilisations in outer space · Annihilation of human civilization

In *The Second Machine Age*, Erik Brynjolfsson and Andrew McAffee (2014) start their considerations from a Fig. 1.1 (page 5), entitled blithely "numerically speaking, most of human history is boring". The Figure depicts the dependence of the number of people on Earth and a human social development index on time during the last 10,000 years and is quoted after (Morris 2010). This dependence is flat and close to zero for almost all 10,000 years and changes into a needle-like development during the last 300 years. Neither Morris, nor Brynjolfsson and McAfee recognise what such graph really means, perhaps because they are not specialists in the dynamics of processes with positive feedback. And what such graph really means is the inevitability of a sharp end of the process by "hitting the ceiling".

For it is almost sure that the avalanche-like development that we observe in human civilization during the last three centuries will end in "hitting the ceiling", encountering a sharp constraint. Such opinion is based on a deep understanding of the dynamics of processes with feedback. The development observed during the last centuries contains, as mentioned in Chap. 3, positive feedback loops. Actually, it is based on two positive feedback loops (Wierzbicki 2015): the first one is the feedback between science and technology (science gives technology new theories to exploit, technology gives science new tools and ideas), the second is the feedback between technology and market (the more money is brought by market application of a new technological idea, the more will be given for further development of this and similar technological ideas). Positive feedbacks result in an avalanche-like development—but this development lasts only as long as it does not encounter a constraint, hence the metaphor of "hitting the ceiling". It was already mentioned that a basic example of a process with positive feedback is snow avalanche, even if it ends not by "hitting the ceiling", and hits the opposite slope instead. Such phenomena are well known in technology: e.g., the dynamics of flip-flop switches, basic elements of old versions of computer memory, was based on positive feedback and constraints—and we, information technologists, had to study this dynamics in order to determine the maximal rate of switching, limiting the speed of operation of computers.

Moreover, contemporary cosmic explorations indicate rather a rarity of such phenomena in the universe as an intelligent civilization. This is described in *The Eerie Silence: Renewing Our Search for Alien Intelligence* (Davies 2010). Davies asks why after at least 50 years of sending radio signals into space, indicating the existence of an intelligent civilization on Earth, we have not yet receive any response? There are many possible answers to the question formulated by Davies but all of them indicate a rarity of intelligent civilizations in the universe, and the most worrying answer is as follows: *civilizations such as ours are rare in space since they are doomed to self-annihilation because of an avalanche-like development.* Therefore, the philosopher Joseph Agassi was quite right when he indicated the most important philosophical problems for future studies (in Olsen and Selinger 2007) by stating that *the most important philosophical problem of today is what we should do to prevent the extinction of human (and other) life on our planet.*

Personally, I hope that humankind will not surrender passively to its fate; however, we should be aware of the danger and look for countermeasures, as suggested by Agassi. This is the purpose of this and the next chapter: this chapter describes one of many possible scenarios of extinction of life on Earth, the next one looks for methods of counteraction.

The scenario presented here is based on the assumption that we do not modify the contemporary capitalism on time, accepting the "elastic labour market", or in fact—the arbitrary licence of employers to determine employment conditions. It is assumed, moreover, that two current megatrends will be upheld: the megatrend of universal betterment of education and the megatrend of minimization of the costs of work (based, in the beginning, on the transfer of work to countries of lower labour costs, however later on automation and robotization). All this will lead to a further increase in the number of well-educated but unsustainably employed precariat. In 40 years, it will amount to over a half of the global working force.

Traditional economy and sociology maintain (see, e.g., Bauman 2000) that there is no problem here: industrial society transforms into service society and most people will find work in services. However, from the time of invention or rather the construction of the first industrial robot (in 1957) many years have passed, and robots are not seen on the streets, as the process of universal social penetration of robots has not yet started (this *delay time* between the invention and the start of a broad social penetration lasted for mobile telephony from 1943 to 1990, thus 47 years; for robots, it might be longer). Thus, when a broad social penetration of mobile robots is started and their prices sufficiently decrease, the work of people in supermarkets—and gradually also in other services—will be cheaply substituted by robots. Therefore, if we do not limit "the elastic labour market", the work of people in services will be marginalized as well, except perhaps for profession that require personal contact, such as teaching (electronic distant education helps in education wide-spreading, but does not replace personal contact) or health services (intelligent diagnostic systems help physicians, but will not replace their intuition; on the other hand, nurses can be replaced by robots).

Demographers (not traditional, but contemporary ones; the impact of education on demography was appreciated first around 1990 due to the work of Warren Sanderson in IIASA[1]) maintain that the increasing share of well-educated women results in a diminishing of their childbearing indexes. Hence, the contemporary predictions of the number of people on the globe indicate that this number will achieve a maximum around 9 billion people around 2050, and later it will stabilize or even slowly diminish. Even if demographic forecasts are the most precise (demographic processes have a very slow and rather simple dynamics), these predictions probably do not take yet into account the impact of the growth of precariat; as mentioned in the former Chapter, precariat delays the moment of having children. However, it is not important here that the demographic global growth will be most probably stopped; what is important are conditions which the huge number of well-educated people will be living in.

The current trends of increasing stratification and inequality, confirmed recently e.g. by a special report *The third great wave* of the weekly The Economist (issue October 4 2014), indicate that there will be conditions of social exclusion in majority of countries. Unable to buy good apartments, precariat will live mostly around future megacities close to slums, and its unemployed part directly in slums. On the other hand, plutocrats will live in closed, strongly guarded enclaves; the protective service for such enclaves will give additional employment for a small part of population, but the impact of general social discontent on these servicemen will be a source of additional dangers.

The universality of multimedia advertisements affecting all people through television integrated with the Internet and mobile telephony will be even more dangerous. Due to the advertisements, precariat will know well in what conditions plutocrats live and what they consume. This will cause an increase of jealousy and revolutionary mood that will be expressed by intensified demonstrations of precariat and riots. Such riots are rather frequent already today, see e.g. (Urbański 2014),

---

[1]International Institute for Applied Systems Analysis in Laxenburg near Vienna, Austria.

even if a more serious clashes of demonstrators with police happen mostly in less developed countries.

Gradually, the price of robots will come down and they will be used much more universally; similarly, there will be less expensive and more universally used software of knowledge engineering and artificial intelligence. In order to avoid conflicts with employees, the owners of supermarkets will replace people with robots; this will spread to other forms of services and will limit sharply the number of working places in services. Knowledge engineering, on the other hand, might replace all routine mental work, such as, e.g., accounting.

If the contemporary principle of "elastic labour market" will be upheld, robots and computers will displace people from a majority of workplaces. New professions will be invented, but employers, having a licence to determine conditions of employment, do not hurry with such inventions; inventing new professions is simply too slow today. A significant decrease in the number of working places will occur during the next 40–50 years, since the processes of socio-economic penetration of new technologies last that long, see (Wierzbicki 2015). Even if the inventions of a robot and artificial intelligence occurred rather long ago, both these technologies still wait for a beginning of a real and broader social penetration; we do not yet see robots walking on the streets or working in the supermarkets. Coupled in a feedback with the principle of "elastic labour market", these technologies pose a kind of a "ticking time bomb" that, when it will explode, will displace people from working places in a rapid manner. Additionally, new technologies will contribute to deepening of conflicts resulting from socio-economic stratification, e.g., new implants of biomedical engineering will be initially available only to the richest layers of society, which will be an additional source of jealousy and frustration.

Hence, precariat will grow even faster and will be well educated, since only well-educated people will have chances for good work. A truly good education will be expensive, but parents will nevertheless try to invest in the education of their children; the poorest and the most talented children will use the Internet and education offered as part of free access. Additionally, governments will promote additional education in their programs fighting unemployment. However, the possibilities of finding good and sustainable work will be scarce even for the best-educated people and this will lead to frustration and growth of revolutionary moods, even in the richest countries.

In the first instance, the well-educated precariat will use the Internet to discuss its situation, part of precariat will propose reforms of the social system and capitalism, but if politicians will not recognise the need of such reforms, the more radical part of precariat will start to organize revolution. This can be done also with the use of the Internet, since more radical hackers often sympathize with anarchistic or revolutionary opinions, and they will develop protected software for revolutionary discussion groups, signalling attempts to break into them. Obviously, no protection can be effective against personal infiltration by agents of governmental intelligence service. Politicians will be informed about the actions of revolutionary groups and will look for palliatives such as raises of minimal salary or educational

6 A Possible Scenario of Annihilation

programs for professions offering more chances of finding work. However, if they will not fully appreciate the seriousness of the situation, they will still avoid more radical reforms of capitalism.

Among such revolutionary groups fractions that postulate more radical actions, such as an international agreement of precariat (or even a new *International of Precariat*) always emerge, preparing a global revolution, trials of strength by demonstrations even in the richest countries. Thus, such demonstrations will be intensified and during one of them the following chain of events can occur—a random concatenation, but history is in its details random, and such random events can lead today to a global nuclear catastrophe.

One of participants of such radical demonstration in the USA will persuade their colleagues to take pitchforks with them "in case police will attack us" (see Hanauer 2014). Police will actually attack, but using CS gas, which will end in dispersing the demonstration, but also enrage its more radical participants. They will form a smaller group that will attack more luxurious cars by puncturing their tires. In one of these cars a family—wife and daughter—of a prominent politician might be travelling, returning from a visit to friends in a strongly guarded housing enclave to their own enclave; the car will be guarded by two armed bodyguards. After the tires of their car are pierced, the bodyguards will use their guns, severely wounding some of demonstrators, which will only further infuriate the others. They will break the windows of the car and pull out all passengers and bodyguards, killing them on the spot with pitchforks.

The prominent politician will learn about this from a report of intelligence service (including the photographs of blooded corpses of his wife and daughter). The report will also stress that the idea of taking pitchforks on the demonstration came from a radical revolutionist of Arab origin that is acquainted with revolutionists in the Arab caliphate between Iraq, Turkey and Iran; that man managed to escape after the event to the caliphate. Desperate after losing his family, the prominent politician will use his prerogatives to initiate a nuclear attack on the caliphate. Accidentally, one of the rockets will hit the territory of Iran which (having slightly less effective intelligence service) will interpret this as an attack from Israel and strike back using nuclear missiles. A better intelligence service in Russia will result in a Russian nuclear attack on the USA; but China will see a chance of gaining Siberia and will hit Moscow with their nuclear rockets.

A world war started in that way, with a mass use of nuclear weapons, will soon end in a nuclear contamination of all our planet. Some plutocrats will try to escape to New Zealand. This country, however, will soon close its borders to immigrants, which will not help much, because clouds of nuclear dust will penetrate the atmosphere of entire Earth. Billions of human population will die suffering; destruction will also engulf all overland fauna and flora, and only some fish species will survive. It will be the end of intelligent civilization on Earth.

Obviously, many other scenarios are possible. The demonstrations and protests of precariat might grow gradually, even if dispersed by police; an international program, coordinated by the Internet, of such demonstrations might emerge. Inevitably, more radical fractions will appear and one of them might commence a garage production of nuclear weapons using the knowledge of the educated precariat (for example, a disenchanted physicist who could not find employment corresponding to his aspirations). Anyway, the amount of nuclear weapons already assembled on Earth, and also the knowledge how to construct such weapons are too dangerous to allow an escalation of social conflicts.

Equally obviously, it is easy to criticize such scenarios. One can point out that both demonstrators and prominent politicians will surely show more good sense and constraint; however, such is a speculation of people who have never lived through the atrocity of a revolution or a charge of a frantic crowd. Personally, I know this only from family history, but, both in the time of the revolution of 1917 in Russia and during mass murder of Poles in 1943 on Volyn, assaults of bloodthirsty crowds on "others" were frequent and an appeal to good sense would not help at all. Similarly, it is difficult to count on good sense in the use of nuclear weapons, since most of catastrophes in nuclear power plants (e.g., in Chernobyl) resulted from the lack of it.

One could criticize such scenarios in the hope that the situation of precariat will not deteriorate to such extent, that revolutionary mood will not be that popular. For example, *The Economist*, in its special report *The third great wave* admittedly acknowledges that "to those that have shall be given" (meaning that new technologies will enrich the richest), but then it downplays this by saying that it always happened so with new technologies from the time of industrial revolution, and new technologies have always replaced some old professions. *The Economist*, however, evidently does not have any knowledge about the dynamics of processes with positive feedback and does not have any inkling of what can be brought in the next several decades by the ticking time bomb of popular robotization and the use of knowledge engineering or artificial intelligence. The opinions of *The Economist* can be paraphrased as follows: we are caught by a snow avalanche and the plutocrats succeeded in taking places on the top it, hence they tell the others (to those who are rolled around inside the avalanche) what a wonderful ride they have—not thinking of how it will end.

Therefore, we cannot prevent such scenarios by invoking good sense, only by turning off the ticking time bomb. This cannot be achieved by prohibiting work on knowledge engineering, artificial intelligence and robotics, we must switch off the detonator, "elastic labour market", by sharply and significantly intensifying labour legislation.

References

Bauman, Z. (2000). *Liquid modernity*. Cambridge: Polity.
Brynjolfsson E., & McAffee A. (2014). *The second machine Age: work, progress and prosperity in a time of brilliant technologies*. New York: W.W. Norton & Co.
Davies, P. (2010). *The eerie silence: Renewing our search for alien intelligence*. Houghton Mifflin Harcourt: New York.
Hanauer N. (2014) The pitchforks are coming … for us plutocrats. *POLITICOMAGAZINE*, July/August 2014.

Morris, J. (2010). *Why the west rules—for now. The patterns of history, and what they reveal about future*. New York: Farrar, Straus and Giroux.

Olsen, J.-K. B., & Selinger, E. (2007). *Philosophy of technology: 5 questions*. UK: Automatic Press.

The Economist. (2014). The third great wave. Special Report. October 4th, 2014.

Urbański, J. (2014). *Prekariat i nowa walka klas (In Polish, The precariat and a new class struggle)*. Warsaw: Instytut Wydawniczy Książka i Prasa.

Wierzbicki, A. P. (2015). *Technen: Elements of recent history of information technologies with epistemological conclusions*. Heidelberg: Springer.

Chapter 7
A Vision of Informed Society and a Sustainable Redistribution System

Abstract This chapter discusses one of possible ways of preventing the catastrophic consequences of the end of work discussed in the previous chapter. The society should be better informed what really happens in global economy under the impacts of next three waves of informational revolution in order to convince, in a democratic way, the politicians about the necessity of more radical reforms of capitalism. Without such reforms, two positive feedback loops between science and technology and between technology and market will result in further avalanche-like development that must end in "hitting the ceiling". One of possible reforms is to provide for a negative feedback in the mechanism of capital replacing labour by introducing a substantial taxation of the incomes of enterprises, combined with strong tax reliefs related to creation of new working places, measured by the part of enterprise income that is spent on labour salaries. Such reform would require an international agreement, but has the advantage that it would provide for a sustainable redistribution system.

Keywords Radical reforms of capitalism · Negative versus positive feedback · Capital replacing labour · Creation of new working places · Degressive taxation · Sustainable redistribution

The scenario discussed earlier may not happen, if society is not only better educated—because it will be—but also *better informed* about what really happens, as distinct from what is pumped into our heads by neoliberal economy in order not to hinder the capitalists in doing what they wish (because they are allegedly wiser than other people). There are many examples of such propaganda: the slogan of "elastic labour market" that really means an arbitrary licence for employers; the special report *The third great wave* of the weekly *The Economist* (2014), illustrated by a vision of a robot entangled in red tape; a recent Polish book by Leszek Balcerowicz (2014) defending neoliberal positions (it does not mention that Joseph Stiglitz has recently won the Nobel price for a critique of neoliberal economy, and tries again to convince Poles that the only way for Poland was the shock therapy).

© The Author(s) 2016
A.P. Wierzbicki, *The Future of Work in Information Society*,
SpringerBriefs in Economics, DOI 10.1007/978-3-319-33909-2_7

Being better informed should also mean a better understanding of contemporary technology and process dynamics, both for technical and social processes. This cannot be achieved without an essential change of the curricula at universities. Technical studies introduced obligatory social and humanity courses, such as economics, sociology, philosophy, already 50 years ago. From this time we, technologists, have been waiting in vain for reciprocity. Indeed, during last decades the *informational revolution* became sufficiently visible and some faculties introduced additional courses on foundations of computer science (persistently naming this revolution *digital* or *IT revolution*, which only shows how deep is its misapprehension). However, for a good understanding of what will be yet brought by contemporary technology, we need not only courses of advanced computer science (together with knowledge engineering or artificial intelligence), but also two other courses: control engineering with robotics and bioengineering.

Control engineering and robotics are important not only because robots can replace most service work during the next 50 years, so they should be well understood. What is more important is a good understanding of the functioning of feedbacks and process dynamics; both are fundamental for control engineering. On the other hand, bioengineering is necessary for several other reasons. Firstly, the global human population is getting older, and old people will be using diverse services of biomedical engineering. Secondly, diverse implants—technical additions to human organism—will be used increasingly often. Thirdly, future medicine will be increasingly dependent on biomedical engineering, together with knowledge engineering applied to aid diagnoses.

These three technological courses correspond to the *three waves* of socio-economic penetration of new technology that have not fully started yet, but are inevitable. The knowledge taught in these courses will be thus necessary for a good understanding of future world. Obviously, philosophy, sociology and economics are also needed, but in a new interpretation, since, e.g. philosophy explains the world falsely if it refers to the so-called paradoxes of vicious circle, self-support and the hydra of infinite regress not knowing that all these paradoxes are ostensible, that they are all some aspects of feedback relation, thus vicious circle and self-support occur millions of times in every computer while each robot works by using infinite regress. Similarly, these sciences tend to interpret logics falsely (a classic example how dangerous it is was the not only erroneous, but also logically faulty slogan "there is no third way"). Technology has applied multivalued logics (that is a contribution of the Polish science, see Łukasiewicz 1911) since long ago and Zdzisław Pawlak, an engineer and constructor of the first Polish computers, proved, in his theory of rough sets, that it is not allowed to exclude middle in large data sets, that there is always some third way (Pawlak 1991).

The global society must be better informed in order to convince, in a democratic way, the politicians about the necessity of more radical reforms of capitalism. Without such reforms, two positive feedback loops between science and technology (science gives technology new theories, technology gives science new tools and ideas in return) and between technology and market (technology gives market new artefacts, market gives technology money for further development of such artefacts that provide market with largest profits) will result in further ava-lanche-like development that must end in "hitting the ceiling".

Such reforms are necessary in order to forestall negative impacts of the already formed (and coming) three waves of socio-economic penetration of new technologies: the use of human-like, mobile robots in all service work (and also in mining); the use of knowledge engineering or artificial intelligence for all routine mental work; the use of biomedical engineering combined with computer science and knowledge engineering in health service and for lengthening the human life. The example of the last wave enables us to show how its course might depend on the socio-economic strategy of its use.

We can imagine at least two opposite strategies of using biomedical engineering. First, aimed at pure profit maximization, will start with very high prices for products of bioengineering; only plutocrats will be able to afford such products to prolong their youth, health and life. However, media will also earn well thanks to the advertisements of such products, and thus precariat will be fully aware of what plutocrats possess; this will arouse bitterness and hatred. The other extreme will be a strategy pro-socially inclined and preferring products helping the eldest and ill, with consciously limited prices; then the products of bioengineering will become popular without large social resistance.

These three waves, and especially the first two of them, will result, however, in the end of work we know today. Should further advancements of mechatronics result in mobile robots cheapening to a similar extent as it has already happened with computers or mobile telephones, then capitalism will obviously replace human work in mining or generally also in services with robots. Therefore, before the waves will spread universally, we must bring about ways to accelerate inventing new professions and new forms of work. This can be done by a fundamental reform of the social redistribution system, *by making the profits of capitalists dependent on the degree of fulfilment of their fundamental duty: creating new working places and their up keeping.*

The new redistribution system must obviously fulfil some fundamental conditions such as are today implemented in countries where quality of life is high (Scandinavian countries or Japan). These conditions include ensuring sufficiently good financing of retirement and other pensions, aid for the unemployed and socially excluded, health service, education and science. A separate question that requires appropriate statistical analysis is the share of such financing in the GDP; in that we must not yield to neoliberal propaganda that tries to limit this share as far as possible. For an approximation I will assume here that today, such a reasonable share amounts to 30–40 %, while it might grow in the future—because the employment in the public sector might be an efficient method of preventing the end of work, see, e.g., (Galwas 2014).

However, the main property of the new redistribution system should be the motivation of employers to create new working places and their upkeep. This can be achieved by a *degressive taxation,* with a degression depending not on the amount of income, but on an index describing the results of creation of working places. Such index might be rather simple: it is enough to define the share of employee wages (excluding the wages of executives) in the total revenues of the enterprise; I will denote this index by the letter z. Of course, the definition of total revenues of the enterprise depends on its' character, but the so-called *value added income* might provide a good guidance.

Again, a separate question requiring statistical analysis is the average level of the index z. For an illustration, data concerning the economic situation of Poland in 2010–11 will be quoted here (based on the publication of the Central Statistical Office of Poland, GUS 2012; GUS employment 2012). In 2010, the Gross Domestic Product of Poland amounted to PLN 1369 milliard, and the total revenues of enterprises (higher than the GDP, as the latter only accounts for the so-called added value) amounted to PLN 2397 milliard. The costs of generating them were PLN 2126 milliard, hence the profit (difference) amounted to only 4.2 % of the total revenues. In these revenues, the cost of work—pre-tax salaries— amounted to PLN 221 milliard, only 9.2 %. If we count additional costs related to salaries (social and health insurance contributions paid by the employer), then the total costs of work grow to PLN 261 milliard, hence only 10.9 % of total revenues. Production in Poland is energy-intensive and raw-material-intensive, but according to (Wilmańska 2010), average indexes describing these aspects amount jointly to ca. 25 %, which corresponds to PLN 559 milliard in the costs of energy and raw materials (an amount similar to the costs of goods imported to Poland). Investments in the sector of private enterprises amounted to ca. PLN 101 milliard, only 4.2 % of total revenues. Corporate income tax, CIT, in this sector systematically decreased, and in 2010, it stood at only PLN 27 milliard, hence merely ca. 1.1 % of the total income of enterprises.

All the above data is related to the sector of private enterprises. At the same time, the ratio of total costs of work in the public sector—PLN 124 milliard in pre-tax salaries, which gives PLN 147 milliard together with social and health insurance costs paid by the employer—to the total expenses of this sector, ca. PLN 295 milliard in 2010, amounts to 42.1 % or even 49.7 % with additional costs included.

This coarse image, however, becomes appalling if we analyze it in more detail. The average level of the index $z = 10.9$ % for the entire sector of private enterprises in Poland indicates that this sector creates working places only in a slogan-like manner, while in reality it minimizes the costs of work. Theoretically, the corporate income tax, CIT, amounting to 19 % of profit, is similar to that paid by every salaried person in PIT, or personal income tax. However, PIT is paid on the income counted with severely restricted reliefs, while the way of establishing profit as a taxable base for CIT allows diverse interpretations and tax evasion by artificial increase of costs (e.g., transfer of money abroad under various excuses) and thus decrease of the profit declared; for if the latter boils down to 4.2 % of total revenues, then the tax actually amounts to only ca. 1 % of total revenues. Hence, the sector of private enterprises in Poland is by no means interested in creating working places and does not contribute much to the public finance; according to Kamil Zubelewicz (Zubelewicz 2011) the share of CIT in public sector funding sources amounts only to ca. 1,2 % only. This indicates that the entrepreneurs take full advantage of the neoliberal propaganda that they will flee Poland if they are not treated on especially beneficial terms, and they eagerly prey on these terms. Taxation specialists frequently voice the opinion that the most effective for an entrepreneur are investments in lobbying for beneficial modifications of taxation laws in the parliament.

Still worse, a large portion of costs of the private enterprise sector remains unexplained. The costs of work, raw materials and energy, taxes and profits account together for only ca. 45.2 % of the total reported revenues; what happens with all the rest? Part of it might be expended on outsourcing, but surely it would boost the employment index in a statistics concerning all enterprises? Part of it corresponds to the expenses on work concealed by compelling some workers to leave the enterprise and start own business, the so-called self-employment, with a promise of outsourcing; this way, the enterprise avoids paying social and health insurance costs—but this is only another way of increasing precariat, is it not? Part of it might be channelled for marketing and advertisements, but to devote for this purpose over half of the revenues is surely an exaggeration? Therefore, we might suspect that the explanations are similar phenomena as occur in the privatized high-tech production enterprises or service enterprises in Poland. A large part of revenues is written off as licence fees and technology transfer costs, which allows the owners to transfer hidden profits to other countries. Poland is thus treated as a country of cheap labour that can be exploited while avoiding taxes. Similar situation can probably be observed also in other countries.

Therefore, the system of taxation of enterprises, CIT, should be essentially changed—in such a way that the employers in their own interests would try to well-pay large number of employees—naturally, trying also to use well their work for the benefit of the enterprise, hence inventing new jobs and professions for them. The system should be such that employers would lose on all hasty attempts to minimize the costs of work either through globalization or automation and robotization. If capitalists are well paid because allegedly they are more entrepreneurial and creative, let them use their creativity to prevent the end of work. This can be achieved by a *degressive CIT*—such that the percentage rate of this taxation depends not on the size of the income, but on the employment index z. In order to make avoiding this taxation more difficult, it should relate not to the profit, but total revenues of the enterprise, possibly with sharply defined reliefs making it close to the value added income. The percentage rate of this taxation might result from a general formula:

$$p = \alpha - \beta z \qquad (7.1)$$

where p is the taxation rate, z is the employment index counted as the ratio of the costs of work (excluding the management work) to the total income, α is a parameter, the maximal percentage rate of taxation when the employment index is close to zero, while $\beta \geq 1$ is the coefficient of motivation of the employer. It would suffice to take $\beta = 1$, because then the employer decreases the taxation by the same amount by which that he increases the costs of work, while the latter can be profitably exploited. However, in the Polish conditions we should assume rather $\beta = 1.1$ and $\alpha = 33$ % (in order to discourage employers to further minimize the costs of work); Then, Eq. (7.1) takes a specific form:

$$p = 36\ \% - 1.1z, \text{ if } z < 30\ \%; p = 3\ \%, \text{ if } z \geq 30\ \% \qquad (7.2)$$

which, regarding the statistical data of 2010, would mean that private enterprises in Poland should pay CIT on average amounting to 21 % of their total income—not such a great increase of the taxation rate even if essential when the possible reliefs on the taxable base are sharply limited. If this taxation is paid on the total revenues of enterprises, it would amount in 2010 in Poland right up to PLN 503 milliard, so it would more than double the proceeds of the public sector. There is no doubt, however, that the entrepreneurs will secure various reliefs; e.g. a justified relief would be to exclude from taxable base the costs of work, which would additionally motivate employers to create new working places. The formulae presented here illustrate only a general idea that must be additionally specified in detail. For example, tax offices have bad experience with formulae since they are capable of being diversely interpreted, but the formulae (7.1) or (7.2) might be used to work out appropriate tables of taxation, e.g., with the rule of rounding off the index z to full percentage points.

It should be required, however, that the employment index is counted only concerning basic workers, with the exclusion of the management, but also only with regard to workers on sustainable employment contracts, safeguarded by specific rules. As it is concluded by Stiglitz (2012), the stability of employment is a positive factor for economic growth, because it motivates the workers to a better quality of work.

However, the argument concerning capital outflow from a country that has unfavourable tax conditions is justified: such radical reform of capitalism through a change of principles of CIT cannot be introduced in a single country, it requires an international agreement. After reaching such agreement it is also necessary to impose international sanctions on countries that would like to exploit this situation and function as tax havens. The issues related to necessary measures against diverse forms of tax evasion were excellently analysed by Stiglitz (2012) in *The Price of Inequality,* and they will not be further discussed here.

For these reasons, I do not think that such a reform will occur soon. Gradually, however, the need of such or a similar reform will grow, if the megatrend of minimization of the costs of work is allowed to further influence the global labour situation. This megatrend results from classical profit maximization in conjunction (actually, a feedback) with subsequent waves of dissemination of new technologies that allow to increase profits by minimizing the cost of work. It was shown in the previous chapter how this leads to a growth of well-educated but embittered precariat. I only hope that we will succeed sufficiently early—say, within the next 50 years—in reaching, in a democratic way, an agreement concerning necessary reforms to avoid the scenario of annihilation of human civilization. As shown above, such reforms are possible.

From approximate estimations shown above it also follows that a sustainable system of social redistribution is perfectly possible. All alarmist opinions on the impossibility of sustaining the system of old age pensions, job-seeking allowances, social health care systems etc. result, as we can conclude from the model estimations quoted above, from the aversion of capitalists to paying taxes in a reasonable proportion to that paid by all other people as part of the personal income tax. Should the rules of taxation be similar for legal entities and physical persons, it would be not difficult to increase public sector revenues twice or even trice.

At the same time, it is obvious that there is a need to have an efficiently functioning state to implement such a redistribution system. On the other hand, we cannot fully trust in the efficiency of state and a strengthened civic control is necessary—including e.g. strengthening of direct democracy—to supervise the efficiency both of central and local government units. The details of such a redistribution system (the retirement and pension allowance rates, even their names— e.g., it is better to call an unemployment relief a pension than relief) must be a subject of broad social debate. However, *there is no doubt that the society of Earth—precisely because of the achievements of technology, if exploited for general welfare, and not only for the benefit of capitalists—is at last able to afford such a sustainable redistribution system.*

It is possible to ask a question: very well, but what will the future workers work on, even if employed, if such a large part of work is performed by robots and computers? I have no doubt that employers, caring for their own profits, will find appropriate tasks to be performed by employees. Part of these tasks will be obviously a supervision of robots and computers; another part will be a continuous improvement (even if sometimes only apparent) of products and services in such a way that they could be sold as innovations; yet another one will be continued tracking of the competition and trends on the market, or business intelligence.

Also, there will be a social pressure to reduce work time for people "since robots and computers work for us". Some anthropologists estimate that in primitive civilizations, it was sufficient for people to work 4 h a day to provide for the needs of their families; perhaps, we could return to such proportions of work and leisure. It is important, however, that shortening of the work time should not become a pretext for a general layout of employees or to a general slogan of "outsourcing", transferring the work to smaller enterprises employing people on arbitrary contracts, cheaper and precarious. Should the corporate income taxation depend negatively on the index of durable employment, enterprises will care about this index and outsourcing will not be a better alternative than a sustainable employment in the own enterprise. Additionally, if the sustainable redistribution system secures a personal pension for everybody, there will be always some people who would prefer not to work or find only occasional occupation, remaining in the status of precariat; but in such a system the risk of revolutionary moods will be smaller.

References

Balcerowicz L. (rozmawiała Stremecka M., 2014). *Trzeba się bić. Opowieść biograficzna.* (*We Should Fight. A Biographic Tale*). Published by Czerwone i Czarne, Warsaw.
Galwas B. (2014). Świat po pierwszej dekadzie XXI wieku. Czas na państwo socjalne. (*The Time for a Social State*). *Przyszłość – Świat, Europa, Polska*, 1/2014, pp. 64–86.
GUS. (2012). *Polska w liczbach (Poland in numbers)*. Warsaw: Central Statistical Office of Poland.
GUS employment. (2012). Zatrudnienie i wynagrodzenia w gospodarce narodowej w 2011 roku (*Employment and Renumerations in Polish Economy*). Central Statistical Office of Poland, Warsaw.

Łukasiewicz J. (1911) O wartościach logicznych (On Logical Values). *Ruch Filozoficzny* I 50–59.

Pawlak, Z. (1991). *Rough sets—theoretical aspects of reasoning about data.* Dordrecht: Kluwer.

Stiglitz, J. (2012). *The price of inequality: How today's divided society endangers our future.* New York: Norton & Co.

The Economist (2014) The third great wave. Special Report. October 4th, 2014.

Wilmańska A. (2010) *Raport o stanie sektora małych i średnich przedsiębiorstw w Polsce w latach 2008-2009 (Report on the State of Small and Middle Enterprises in Poland in the Years 2008–2009).* Warsaw: Polska Agencja Rozwoju Przedsiębiorczości.

Zubelewicz K. (2011). Środki sektora finansów publicznych w Polsce w latach 1990–2010 (*Sources of the Public Finance Sector in Poland in the Years 1990–2010*). *Przyszłość: Świat, Europa, Polska* 1/2011, pp. 148–171.

Chapter 8
Who Will Be Adverse?

Abstract This chapter discusses possible objections to the radical reform of capitalism proposed in the previous chapter. The objections might relate to the seemingly utopian character of the proposed reform, might result from the paradigm of predominantly neoliberal economics (while this paradigm does not include an understanding of possible impacts of positive feedbacks), might argue that precariat is a new and untested concept, etc. The Author argues, however, that enterprises are needed in a country mainly for providing working places, and if they do not perform accordingly to this ethical obligation, they should be forced to do so by a suitable taxation system. The proposed reform is obviously a kind of a hybrid of socialism and capitalism, with a market-oriented version of the universal right of work; but most of serious writings about the future of capitalism require such a hybrid solution. The proposed reform cannot be introduced without an international agreement, but such an agreement is needed in order to prevent the danger of annihilation of human intelligence on Earth.

Keywords Positive feedbacks versus neoliberal economics · Ethical duty to create new working places · Why do we need entrepreneurs · A hybrid of socialism and capitalism · Market-oriented version of universal right of work · Dangers of exponential development

Such a radical reform of capitalism will encounter many adversaries: the majority of capitalists, large part of politicians in a close alliance with capitalists, but also more conservative representatives of social sciences, mainly economists who reluctantly abandon old paradigms and patterns of thinking. Therefore, I should present here diverse types of objections that I expect.

Firstly, I expect an objection that all this book is utopian or represents "mythology for the unlearned", as it was expressed by a conservative economist concerning the book of Piketty (2014)—even if the book of Piketty was not futurologist, but based on enormous research material. On the objection of "the unlearned" I would respond that "the pot is calling the kettle black" while it is unlearned itself, e.g., in the field of the dynamics of processes with positive feedback or the dynamics of social penetration of

© The Author(s) 2016
A.P. Wierzbicki, *The Future of Work in Information Society*,
SpringerBriefs in Economics, DOI 10.1007/978-3-319-33909-2_8

the products of new technology. I know mathematical models of econometrics well, have worked myself on game theory and its applications, and know that economic forecasts are applicable only in a short-term horizon, as opposite, e.g., to demography. In order for a long-term forecast to be reliable, it must concern processes of slow and ponderous dynamics, and it always has some utopian features. However, a positive utopia was always an engine of civilization advance (and who does not believe in such advance, should reflect whether he would like to live two hundred years earlier, when the average life span was twice shorter than today). Moreover, as explained in Chap. 2, I believe it is my ethical obligation to present conclusions concerning possible ways of preventing the annihilation of intelligent life on Earth.

Arguments for the thesis that such annihilation is threatening us, at least as a possibility, I presented in Chap. 6. Intelligent civilizations are rare in the universe, and this indicates some conclusions. We are riding caught by a developmental avalanche, caused by two positive feedback loops: between science and technology and between technology and market. I expect also arguments such as presented by The Economist (special report on October 4 2014)—that there is no reason to fear, new technologies always caused social stratification, but this is good because it motivates people, new technologies always replaced labour to some extent, but that is normal and not dangerous. I respond that these are arguments of those who, caught by the avalanche, found themselves by chance on its top and tell other people rolled by what a beautiful ride it is. An avalanche always ends by hitting the opposite slope and on Earth we have gathered too much nuclear weapons and knowledge how to make them to watch impassively the growth of revolutionary atmosphere.

Therefore, we cannot impassively accept right-wing arguments that would not recognize the growth of precariat because any information about it is treated as a sign of alien and unwanted left-wing ideology. Not ideology is important here, but facts; an actual situation concerning the megatrend of minimization of the costs of work and its effects in Poland is illustrated best by the data of Central Statistical Office of Poland, GUS, discussed in detail in Chap. 7.

Obviously, capitalists will not want to pay higher corporate income tax. In the world, disputes as to the amount of taxation are popular, e.g., the republicans in the USA systematically oppose increasing taxation, and small taxation and small state are a fetish in the neoliberal ideology. On the other hand, however, when the prime minister of Sweden—a country that is systematically ranked among the best as regards the quality of life—was asked about the cause of such successes, he answered "because we have large taxes and use them well".

I expect also an argument that "Poland did not have capital, had to induce foreign capital for domestic investments". The answer is: depends what capital and for what purpose. The commercial capital of big supermarkets would anyway come to Poland in order to exploit the big market. The industrial and service capital is needed in Poland to create new working places. Those capitalists who realize well their ethical duty to create work places and achieve the ratio of salary expenditures to the total revenues (the index z) larger than 30 %, would preserve their privileges and be almost entirely free of corporate income tax. Taxation will concern those who minimize the costs of work—and will motivate them reversely to increase these costs. Such taxation will also prevent the employers from increasing the numbers of precariat, e.g., by forcing their workers to start their own "economic activity".

I expect also the argument that such version of corporate income tax, CIT, is a hybrid of capitalism and socialism. Yes, indeed, it is a market-oriented (not absolute) version of the universal right to work. However, I consciously searched for a hybrid that would preserve positive aspects of capitalism and limit its negative aspects. Positive aspects are market economy with its pursuit of efficiency; negative aspects consist in transforming this pursuit into the megatrend of minimizing costs of work. Perhaps there are also other solutions possible, fulfilling such goals. However, I wanted to show that such a hybrid is fully possible and rational. Moreover, the statistical data from Poland imply that accepting the principle of corporate income tax, CIT, being paid in a similar proportion to personal income tax, PIT, would provide the state with a sufficient budgetary income to upkeep a sustainable redistribution system, including fair old age pensions, decent allowances for the disabled and unemployed, well-financed health care, science and education. Neoliberal stories arguing that such a system is not sustainable express only the unwillingness to pay CIT in a fair proportion.

We can also expect the objection that an universal right to work will create inefficiency of work and market shortages. Indeed, but only if treated absolutely, as evidenced by the history of real socialism. In a combination with labour market, where the employer selects efficient workers, such effect is improbable. For example in China, where a universal right to work is implemented as part of a market system, such effect is not visible.

Such a hybrid has also the advantage of sustaining the economic demand foundations of capitalism. Excessive stratification and socio-economic exclusion would destroy the demand observed today, since plutocrats create a demand which is highly specific and actually socially insignificant, What is necessary is large demand generated by the middle class and lower layers of society, when a redistribution system provides them with sufficient income.

It is also obvious that invoking the ethical duty of capitalists will not suffice alone, and that capital (at least industrial and service-oriented, and not commercial capital) would escape from a country had it introduced such a reform on its own. Thus, an international agreement, at least between the majority of developed countries, is necessary in order to introduce a degressive corporate income tax, CIT, high for fully-automated work and decreasing with the increase of the employment index. Agreement of that requires time and convincing the majority of politicians that such a reform is truly necessary.

However, the majority of politicians, even if they care for the results of the next elections, usually yields to the opinions of capitalists—because the latter can hire diverse experts, professionals and lobbyists, can also directly help in financing of political parties. Therefore, convincing politicians that such a reform is truly needed might succeed only under a long-term pressure of the society, eliminating politicians that would not perceive the necessity of such reform in elections.

And such pressure will gradually grow, together with the growth of the number and education level of precariat, and with the escalation of social conflicts related to it. Moreover, even if the demonstrations of precariat, or generally social unrest and "new class struggle" (see, e.g., Urbański 2014), will gradually intensify, also a collective social consciousness is necessary that such a hybrid of capitalism and socialism is possible and desired, and that it suffices to introduce a reform of the corporate income tax, CIT.

The slowness of the process of social and international acceptation of such a hybrid means that we should not expect politicians of many countries to perceive the need of corresponding reforms earlier than in a dozen years and achieve an international agreement earlier than in several dozen years. We should only hope that none of possible annihilation scenarios will be realized earlier than that. Counteracting such scenarios requires also strengthening of international cooperation—either by increasing the prerogatives of United Nations, or utilization of other global organizations. This does not mean a global government yet—even if the acceleration of globalization processes indicates such a need—but strengthening of cooperation in the face of growing global hazards.

An international agreement will not occur fast, since some countries might seek advantage in playing off the interests of international capital for their own benefit—by offering a more advantageous condition of CIT than other countries. This is also a standard form of taxation evasion by the international capital—playing off the interests of diverse countries while encouraging them to provide tax reliefs for that capital, see (Stiglitz 2012). We should take, however, into account the opinion of Josef Stiglitz that such divisions endanger our common future; in his book, Stiglitz presents many ways of counteracting them.

Therefore, I present here an opinion that even if the end of capitalism known today is necessary, nevertheless there exists a chance of rather small reform of capitalism, modifying it slightly in the direction of some elements of socialism, of an universal right of work treated not absolutely, but within a market-oriented implementation. Such a reform might secure the survival both of capitalism and of human civilization. It will also mean that *even in the conditions of advanced informational revolution, in a society where robots and knowledge engineering are widespread, we will not run short of work and the possibility of self-fulfilment.*

References

Piketty, Th. (2014). *Capital in the twenty-first century.* Cambridge Mass: Harvard University Press.

Stiglitz, J. (2012). *The price of inequality: How today's divided society endangers our future.* New York: Norton & Co.

The Economist (2014) The third great wave. Special report. October 4th, 2014.

Urbański, J. (2014). *Prekariat i nowa walka klas (The Precariat and a New Class Struggle).* Warsaw: Instytut Wydawniczy Książka i Prasa.

Chapter 9
Final Conclusions

Abstract This chapter presents conclusions of the book in a concise form. Although precise forecasting is impossible, an approximate forecasting is necessary. The end of work will occur, if the slogan of elastic labour market will be uphold, resulting in a continued positive feedback in the mechanism of capital replacing labour. We are already observing a global megatrend of minimization of the cost of work; next three waves of informational revolution will accelerate this megatrend. In order to counteract the end of work, we need a negative feedback stabilizing the effects of the positive ones. Such a feedback might be achieved by a degressive taxation of the incomes of enterprises, decreasing with the increased ratio of labour salaries in the income. This might be an essential reform of capitalism, but it has twofold advantage. It provides for creation of new professions and new working places together with stimulating mass demand that is a foundation of the capitalist system. Moreover, it provides for a sustainable redistribution system. However, such a reform requires an international agreement which will probably take much time.

Keywords End of work—inevitable or not? · Dangers of elastic labour market · Megatrend of minimizing cost of work · Degressive CIT · Creating new professions and working places · Stimulating mass demand · Sustainable redistribution system

The conclusions should begin with a reminder that even if precise forecasting is impossible, an approximate forecasting is necessary and always contributes to civilization development. This book has a futurologist character, although it is based also on scientific premises. Forecasts described here are based on the knowledge of dynamics of the social penetration processes related to the advances of informational technology and dynamics of the processes with positive feedback (Wierzbicki 2015), and also on experience in future studies (Kleiber et al. 2011).

Concerning the question *whether the end of work is imminent*, the answer is twofold. Undoubtedly yes, if we upkeep the impact of the so-called *elastic labour market*, meaning actually the licence of employers to determine the conditions of

© The Author(s) 2016
A.P. Wierzbicki, *The Future of Work in Information Society*,
SpringerBriefs in Economics, DOI 10.1007/978-3-319-33909-2_9

work at their own discretion, which combined with the upcoming waves of informational revolution results in a positive feedback and a *megatrend of minimization of the costs of work*. In other words, the positive feedback between the technology and the market means that the more an employer can exploit information technologies to decrease the costs of work and to increase his own profits, the more he will invest in applications of such technologies. And positive feedbacks result in avalanche-like processes that end in hitting constraints. In this case, the constraint is a full elimination of human work, such as in nuclear explosion the constraint is full disintegration of the atoms of enriched uranium.

Already today we observe a world-wide megatrend of a decrease in the costs of work; in Poland it is expressed in the fact that the costs of work in private enterprises have fallen to only ca. 10 % of the revenues of these enterprises. This happens even if a broad social penetration occurred only for the three first waves of the informational revolution: personal computers, cellular telephony, and the Internet. The next three waves are robots, knowledge engineering (popularly called artificial intelligence) and biomedical engineering; these three waves have already started, but have not yet achieved broad social penetration; robots do not walk with us on the streets nor they work in supermarkets. When it comes to their popular social penetration, these waves, coupled in a positive feedback with profit maximization by capitalists, will lead to an almost full end of work. In this sense Rifkin (1995) was right when he forecasted the end of work, even if he encountered a Cassandra effect: the more precisely one forecasts, the less he is believed.

To control the processes resulting from a positive feedback it is necessary—such as in a nuclear reactor—to limit them by applying an additional negative feedback. Concerning the end of work, it is necessary to additionally motivate employers to increase, and not to decrease the cost of work. This means an introduction of *degressive taxation*, a strong negative dependence of taxation rate of corporate income tax, CIT, on an employment index, calculated as the ratio of total employee salaries (with management remuneration excluded) to the total revenues of the enterprise. This must be connected, however, with an increase of the amount of CIT that was until now avoided by entrepreneurs.

Such a solution has twofold advantage. Firstly, *it preserves the work and employment for majority of people, giving them satisfaction, self-fulfilment and money that will sustain a mass demand that is the foundation of contemporary capitalism.* Secondly, paying corporate income tax, CIT, in a scale comparable to personal income tax, PIT, *will increase the inflows to the public budget and make it possible to secure a sustainable system of income redistribution*, sufficing—despite the alarmist neoliberal warnings—to offer fair old age pensions, pensions for the disabled and unemployed, and sound financing of health service, science and education.

Therefore, such a solution constitutes a seemingly small, but actually rather radical reform of capitalism, it creates a specific hybrid of capitalism and socialism by introducing a version of universal right to work in a market system. It also induces capitalists to fulfil—while caring for their own profits—their ethical duty to create new places of work and new professions.

Such a solution has, however, one fundamental disadvantage: it cannot be introduced in a single country since it would cause a flight of capital to other countries. Thus, an international agreement about such a solution to be introduced in majority of countries is necessary. Therefore, we cannot expect the introduction of such modification of CIT soon.

Nevertheless, such international agreement and such reform of capitalism are necessary. It follows from the fact that the contemporary minimization of the costs of work and the socio-economic stratification resulting from it has led to the emergence of precariat, a social layer (or class) of people employed unsustainably or unemployed. However, precariat becomes better educated in connection with the world-wide megatrend of education bettering, and is more and more aware of its destiny. The unrest and demonstrations resulting from the social exclusion of precariat become increasingly frequent in the world (Urbański 2014). Continuing impact of the minimization of costs of work will result in the growth of the number of precariat, unrests and demonstrations, together with the growth of revolutionary air. A part of capitalists and oligarchs is aware of that, *vide* "the pitchforks are coming for us, plutocrats" (Hanauer 2014).

However, the actual danger is related to the amassment of nuclear weapons and the technology of their construction; a simple accident can result in the escalation of the use of such weapons and the annihilation of intelligent civilization on Earth (it is telling that intelligent civilizations are rare in space). Therefore, it is suicidal to allow an excessive growth of revolutionary atmosphere, particularly related to the unemployment of well-educated people. Thus, a corresponding reform of capitalism and a related international agreement become necessary.

I have written this book in order to show that there exists an effective and realistic method of such a reform, in the hope that the awareness of this fact and of the necessity of the reform will gradually become widespread. For there is no doubt *that the society of Earth—precisely because of the achievements of technology, if only used for general welfare, and not only for the benefit of capitalists—at last enable us to afford such a sustainable redistribution system.*

References

Hanauer N. (2014). *The pitchforks are coming ... for us plutocrats.* POLITICOMAGAZINE, July/August 2014.

Kleiber M,, Kleer, J., Wierzbicki, A. P., Galwas, B., Kuźnicki, L., Sadowski, Z., & Strzelecki Z. (2011). *Report Poland 2050.* Committee for Future Studies at the Presidium of P.Ac.Sc., Warsaw.

Rifkin J. (1995). *The end of work: The decline of the global labor force and the dawn of the post-market era.* Putnam Publishing Group.

Urbański, J. (2014). *Prekariat i nowa walka klas (The Precariat and a New Class Struggle).* Warsaw: Instytut Wydawniczy Książka i Prasa.

Wierzbicki, A. P. (2015). *Technen: Elements of recent history of information technologies with epistemological conclusions.* Heidelberg: Springer.

Index

© The Author(s) 2016
A.P. Wierzbicki, *The Future of Work in Information Society*,
SpringerBriefs in Economics, DOI 10.1007/978-3-319-33909-2